12/25/2011

Dear Linda,

May this book of prayers bless, comfort & strengthen you. The Lord is listening & answering our requests. His Everlasting love to you & mine also.

Jackie

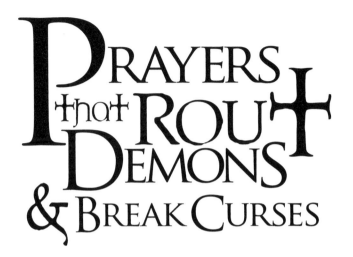

PRAYERS that ROUT DEMONS & BREAK CURSES

JOHN ECKHARDT

CHARISMA
HOUSE

Most CHARISMA HOUSE BOOK GROUP products are available at special quantity discounts for bulk purchase for sales promotions, premiums, fund-raising, and educational needs. For details, write Charisma House Group, 600 Rinehart Road, Lake Mary, Florida 32746, or telephone (407) 333-0600.

PRAYERS THAT ROUT DEMONS/PRAYERS THAT BREAK CURSES
   by John Eckhardt
Published by Charisma House
Charisma Media/Charisma House Book Group
600 Rinehart Road
Lake Mary, Florida 32746
www.charismahouse.com

Unless otherwise noted, all Scripture quotations are from the King James Version of the Bible.

Scripture quotations marked AMP are from the Amplified Bible. Old Testament copyright © 1965, 1987 by the Zondervan Corporation. The Amplified New Testament copyright © 1954, 1958, 1987 by the Lockman Foundation. Used by permission.

Scripture quotations marked NIV are from the Holy Bible, New International Version of the Bible. Copyright © 1973, 1978, 1984, International Bible Society. Used by permission.

Scripture quotations marked ASV are from the American Standard Bible. Copyright © 1960, 1962, 1968, 1971, 1972, 1973, 1975, by the Lockman Foundation. Used by permission.

Scripture quotations marked CEV are from the Contemporary English Version, copyright © 1995 by the American Bible Society. Used by permission.

Scripture quotations marked THE MESSAGE are from The Message: The Bible in Contemporary English, copyright © 1993, 1994, 1995, 1996, 2000, 2001, 2002. Used by permission of NavPress Publishing Group.

Scripture quotations marked NASU are from the New American Standard Bible–Updated Edition, Copyright © 1960, 1962, 1963, 1968,

BOOK 1

PRAYERS that ROUT DEMONS

JOHN ECKHARDT

CONTENTS

I—PLUGGING INTO THE POWER SOURCE

II—PREPARING TO ENGAGE THE ENEMY

III—Confronting the Enemy's Tactics

IV—Destroying the Enemy's Forces

V—EXPERIENCING DELIVERANCE AND RELEASE

FOREWORD

IRST, I WOULD LIKE TO THANK OUR LORD AND SAVIOR
Jesus Christ for giving Apostle John Eckhardt such boldness and love for His people. During the years that I have
known Apostle Eckhardt, I have found him to be a man who
loves God and God's people. He has been found to be faithful
to the Lord, his family, and the ministry. I have observed him
increase in the revelation of God's Word and knowledge of
deliverance. Apostle Eckhardt has never compromised or been
afraid to preach the truth, whereas other pastors would not
address these issues because of losing members and/or money.
His concern is getting God's people free.

I have had many people throughout the years tell me that
Apostle Eckhardt has helped them in many areas of their lives.
There are many testimonies throughout the United States
and all over the world of people being delivered through his
ministry. He has written several books and recorded several
tapes and CDs that have assisted people in getting free from
things that seemed hopeless. Personally, I can say that Apostle
Eckhardt's ministry has been a blessing to me.

Apostle Eckhardt has a special anointing and the wisdom
to put such awesome and powerful warfare prayers together to
enlighten and equip the body of Christ. This book is powerful
on impact and is guaranteed to help in every area of your life.
Often times people are bound by witchcraft and curses but
do not know how to be free. Whereas most Christians are
unaware of curses that affect their lives, Apostle Eckhardt's
book reveals curses and how to break the curses and bind
the enemy. This book gives you the prayers that break every

demonic stronghold on your life. Upon reading these prayers, the power of God will set you free from witchcraft, curses, and idolatry, and healing will be loosed in your life. This book deals with remedies for overthrowing the powers of darkness and principalities and for breaking curses on your land. The same prayers could be used for your city. Also, these prayers will get the dark areas out of your life so that God can use you in greater ways. After breaking the curse, Apostle Eckhardt teaches you how to loose blessings over yourself and your family. If you have ever desired the fire of God in your life, this book teaches you how to release the fire of the living God to preach, prophesy, heal the sick, and cast out devils.

This book is a must-have for every believer.

—RUTH BROWN
Author, *Destroying the Works of Witchcraft
Through Fasting & Prayer*

INTRODUCTION

P*RAYERS* T*HAT* R*OUT* D*EMONS* COMBINES PRAYER AND confession of the Word of God to bring breakthrough against any demonic opposition. Prayer and confession of the Word are two of the most powerful weapons believers have. You will see a great release of God's power when these two are combined.

I began writing these prayers as I studied the Word of God. The Holy Spirit illuminated many scriptures to me that needed to be released through prayer. I began to see clearly the plan of God for believers and how the enemy wanted to stop that plan. The Lord taught me the importance of praying the Word to overcome spiritual resistance to the plan of God for my life.

These prayers have been forged over a period of many years. They have been birthed out of warfare and deliverance. They have come from years of experience in ministering to individuals and nations. The Holy Spirit has helped me understand many scriptures and how to use them in prayer.

Most of the prayers in this book will have Scripture references. We base our prayers on the Word of God. The Word of God will inspire you to pray. The promises of God will motivate you to pray. God has given us many great and precious promises. It is through faith and patience we inherit the promises (Heb. 6:12).

There are many believers who struggle with prayer. Many say they don't know how to pray. Some have become discouraged in prayer. This book will help you learn how to pray with revelation and authority. These prayers are designed to see results. We have received many testimonies of people coming to another level in their prayer lives by using these prayers. They are written to be simple, yet powerful.

There are many different kinds of prayers in this book. We are told to pray with all kinds of prayers (Eph. 6:8). These prayers will expand your ability to pray. You will pray many different kinds of prayers that you ordinarily would not have prayed. This will help to break the limitations off of your prayer life.

Prayer is one of the ways we release the will of God upon the earth. We must study the Word of God in order to know the will of God. This is why prayer and the Word must be combined. Daniel was able to pray effectively because he knew the Word of God concerning His people (Dan. 9:2–3).

We should pray with understanding (1 Cor. 14:15). Understanding the will of God will help us pray correctly. The Word of God is the will of God. We are not to be unwise, but understanding of what the will of the Lord is (Eph. 5:17). Prayer also helps us walk perfectly and completely in all the will of God (Col. 4:12).

Life and death are in the power of the tongue (Prov. 18:21). Right words are forcible (Job 6:25). The words we speak are spirit and life (John 6:63). We can be snared by the words of our mouth. We need to articulate the thoughts of God by praying and confessing His Word (Isa. 55:8). God's Word released through our tongue will cause His power to manifest in our lives.

Words are used to convey our thoughts. The words of God are the thoughts of God. We are releasing the mind of God when we pray and confess His Word. The thoughts of God are peace and prosperity (Jer. 29:11). They are designed to bring us to an expected end.

Jesus taught us that our faith is released through our words (Mark 11:23). Our faith-filled words can move mountains. There is nothing impossible to those who believe. Our faith is a key to seeing miracles and breakthrough on a consistent basis. Whatever we ask in prayer, believing, we will receive (Matt. 21:22).

The Word is near us (Rom. 10:8). The Word is in our mouth and heart. This is the Word of faith. The mouth and the heart are connected. We speak from the abundance of the heart. The Word of God in our heart will come through our mouth. Faith in the heart will be released through our mouth. God watches over His Word to perform it (Jer. 1:12).

We are encouraged to call upon the Lord. He has promised to show us great and mighty things (Jer. 33:3). The Lord delights in our prayers. He delights in answering our prayers. Before we call, He will answer (Isa. 65:24). The Lord's ears are open to the prayers of the righteous (1 Pet. 3:12). The effectual, fervent prayer of a righteous man avails much (James 5:16). We are told to pray without ceasing (1 Thess. 5:17).

Our God hears prayer. All flesh should come to Him in prayer (Ps. 65:2). This book is designed for believers in any nation. All believers have similar challenges. All believers must overcome these challenges. God is no respecter of persons. He is near to all who call upon Him (Ps. 145:19). The Lord will hear your supplication and will receive your prayer (Ps. 6:9).

Calling upon the Lord will bring salvation and deliverance from your enemies (Ps. 18:3). This has always been a key to deliverance. You can pray yourself out of any adverse situation. The Lord is your helper. God will not turn away your prayer (Ps. 66:20). God will not despise your prayer (Ps. 102:17). The prayer of the upright is God's delight (Prov. 15:8).

We have been given the keys of the kingdom (Matt. 16:19). This gives us the authority to bind and loose. *To bind* means "to restrict, stop, hinder, fetter, check, hold back, arrest, or put a stop to." *To loose* means "to untie, unbind, unlock, liberate, release, forgive, or free." Keys represent the authority to lock (bind) or unlock (loose). Prayer and confession are two of the ways we use this authority. We can bind the works of darkness, which include: sickness, disease, hurt, witchcraft, poverty, death, destruction, confusion, defeat, and discouragement. We can loose ourselves and others from the works of darkness. This will result in greater liberty and prosperity.

Binding and loosing will help us in the area of deliverance. We can loose ourselves from many things by using our authority. We can loose others by praying these prayers. Jesus came to destroy the works of the devil. He came that we might have life in abundance.

Believers must know and operate in authority. Jesus gave His disciples power and authority over all devils (Matt. 10:1). We are seated with Christ in heavenly places far above all principality and power (Eph. 1:20–21; 2:6). Believers can use this authority through prayer and confession. We have authority to tread upon serpents and scorpions (Luke 10:19). Jesus promised that nothing would hurt us. Many believers suffer unnecessarily because they fail to exercise their authority.

These prayers are for believers who have a hatred for the works of darkness (Ps. 139:21). Do you hate every false way (Ps. 119:104)? Do you want to see changes in your city, region, and nation? You are a king, and you have the power to change geographic regions (Eccles. 8:4). The fear of the Lord is to hate evil (Prov. 8:13).

The prayers in this book are designed to demolish strongholds. God's Word is like a hammer that breaks the rock in pieces (Jer. 23:29). We need powerful prayers to demolish these strongholds. These prayers are for those who want to see breakthroughs in their personal lives as well as in their cities, regions, and nations. There have been many prayer books written over the years, but I believe this prayer book is unique in its simplicity and revelation.

Satan has been defeated through the cross. Principalities and powers have been spoiled (Col. 2:15). We are enforcing this victory through our prayers. We are executing the judgments written. This honor is given to all His saints. The saints have possessed the kingdom (Dan. 7:18). This means we have authority with the King to advance the reign of Christ over the nations.

David was a king who understood the place of prayer in victory. He had many victories over his enemies. He saw mighty deliverance through prayer. He prayed for the defeat of his enemies, and God answered him. We will have the same results over our spiritual enemies. We are not wrestling against flesh and blood. We must overcome principalities and powers with the armor of God. We must take the sword of the Spirit and pray with all prayer (Eph. 6:12–18).

The prayers of David ended with Psalm 72:20. He ended them by praying that the whole earth would be filled with God's glory. This is the end of prayer. We believe that the earth will be filled with the knowledge of the glory of the Lord as the waters cover the sea (Hab. 2:14). This is our goal. We will continue to pray toward the fulfillment of this promise. We will see the growth of God's kingdom and the destruction of the powers of darkness through our prayers. Revival and glory are increasing. Our prayers are like gasoline to the fire.

SECTION 1

PLUGGING into the POWER SOURCE

OUR SOURCE OF POWER IS THE HOLY SPIRIT AND THE Word of God. We build ourselves up in faith when we confess the Word of God. We experience greater confidence when we understand the Word and walk in revelation. Prayer plugs us into the power source. Prayer connects us to God and allows His power to flow to us in any situation.

Salvation is the basis for warfare. The new birth is a necessity. A believer also needs the infilling of the Holy Spirit. Are you born again? Do you know beyond a doubt that you are saved? Believers must live holy lives that are submitted to the Holy Spirit. We are commanded to walk in the Spirit. This will assure us of continual victory and breakthroughs for others. We can avenge disobedience when our obedience is fulfilled. Jesus cast out devils through the power of the Holy Spirit (Matt. 12:28). The Holy Spirit was the source of His power and wisdom.

This section of prayers that teach us how to plug into the power source—God's Holy Spirit and God's Word—is not for religious people. These are not religious prayers that begin to work when someone recites them. These prayers are for born-again believers who desire to see the growth of the kingdom of God.

We are told to be strong in the Lord and in the power of His might (Eph. 6:10). We walk and war in His strength. This

1

requires humility and total dependence upon God. We are not confident in our own strength. We cannot allow pride to open the door for destruction.

The Lord is a man of war (Exod. 15:3). He will fight our battles. We depend upon His power and direction. We depend upon His Word and His Spirit. I cannot overemphasize the need for humility. God gives grace to the humble.

The Lord is the strength of my life. This gives me the ability to overcome all fear. I will put my trust in Him. This was the key to David's victories. David was a king who knew how to depend upon the Lord. David won many battles and overcame all of his enemies.

The Lord taught David how to war (Ps. 144:1). He will also teach you how to war. You must depend on Him. The prayers and strategies in this book were learned from years of warring and trusting in God. God taught us how to war using His Word. The Holy Spirit opened our eyes to great truths, and we are still learning.

God was David's power source. He confessed that the Lord was his strength. David was a man of prayer and worship. He enjoyed the Lord's presence. The Lord's presence was David's source of joy and strength. His songs were powerful prophetic weapons against the enemy. There is no substitute for a life of praise and worship. Every believer needs to belong to a church that is strong in praise and worship.

There are many great warriors being trained in the school of the Holy Spirit. They are humble people who had to depend upon God for breakthrough. They had to connect with the Lord, who is the greatest warrior. They learned through experience and sometimes through failure. Like these great warriors for God, if we call upon the Lord, He will show us great and mighty things.

The Word of God is the sword of the Spirit. A sword is used in war. The Lord will teach you how to use this sword. You will use it against the spiritual enemies of your soul. You will see great victories as you use it correctly. Most of the prayers in this book have a Scripture reference. I would encourage you to look at the verses and meditate on them. The Word of God is our source of wisdom. We operate in God's wisdom to defeat the powers of hell.

Confessing the Word of God is an important part of every believer's spiritual life. Christianity is called *the great confession*. Salvation comes from confessing with the mouth. The mouth is connected to the heart. The Word of God released from your mouth will be planted in your heart. Faith is released from the mouth. The mouth can only release what is in the heart. Faith in the heart that is released through the mouth can move mountains.

God is the source of all our victories and breakthrough. He is the source of our wisdom and strategies. His Word is the source for our understanding of the warfare in which we are involved. Our warfare originates in the heavens. We bind what is already bound in the heavens. We loose what is already loosed in the heavens.

God has illuminated many scriptures to us over the years of being involved in deliverance and warfare. These scriptures have been invaluable in helping us experience breakthrough. The Word of God is a treasure chest of wisdom and knowledge. It contains an abundance of revelation for every believer. Every believer who desires to enjoy liberty and victory must take time to study the Word of God and ask for revelation.

One of my favorite group of prayers in this section are those called Prayers for Revelation. When I began to pray these prayers, the results were dramatic. I began to see truths in the Word of God that I had never seen. Revelation is the key to authority. Peter received the keys of the kingdom after he received the revelation that Jesus was Christ (Matt. 16:16).

God has promised to make us joyful in the house of prayer (Isa. 56:7). God's house is called a *house of prayer* for all nations. I believe we should not only pray but also enjoy prayer. The joy of the Lord is our strength. Prayer should yield an abundance of miracles and rewards. Those who enjoy the results of prayer will enjoy an exciting life.

Confessions

No weapon formed against me shall prosper, and every tongue that rises against me in judgment I condemn (Isa. 54:17).

I am established in righteousness, and oppression is far from me (Isa. 54:14).

The weapons of my warfare are not carnal but mighty through God to the pulling down of strongholds (2 Cor. 10:4).

I take the shield of faith, and I quench every fiery dart of the enemy (Eph. 6:16).

I take the sword of the Spirit, which is the Word of God, and use it against the enemy (Eph. 6:17).

I am redeemed from the curse of the law. I am redeemed from poverty. I am redeemed from sickness. I am redeemed from spiritual death (Gal. 3:13).

I overcome all because greater is He that is in me than he that is in the world (1 John 4:4).

I stand in the evil day having my loins girded about with truth, and I have the breastplate of righteousness. My feet are shod with the gospel of peace. I take the shield of faith. I am covered with the helmet of salvation, and I use the sword of the Spirit, which is the Word of God (Eph. 6:14–17).

I am delivered from the power of darkness and translated into the kingdom of God's dear Son (Col. 1:13).

I tread upon serpents and scorpions and over all the power of the enemy, and nothing shall hurt me (Luke 10:19).

I do not have the spirit of fear but power, love, and a sound mind (2 Tim. 1:7).

I am blessed with all spiritual blessings in heavenly places in Christ Jesus (Eph. 1:3).

I am healed by the stripes of Jesus (Isa. 53:5).

My hand is upon the neck of my enemies (Gen. 49:8).

You anoint my head with oil; my cup runs over. Goodness and mercy shall follow me all the days of my life (Ps. 23:5–6).

I am anointed to preach, to teach, to heal, and to cast out devils.

I receive abundance of grace and the gift of righteousness, and I reign in life through Christ Jesus (Rom. 5:17).

I have life and that more abundantly (John 10:10).

I walk in the light as He is in the light, and the blood of Jesus cleanses me from all sin (1 John 1:7).

I am the righteousness of God in Christ (2 Cor. 5:21).

I am the head and not the tail (Deut. 28:13).

I shall decree a thing, and it shall be established in my life (Job 22:28).

I have favor with God and with man (Luke 2:52).

Wealth and riches are in my house, and my righteousness endures forever (Ps. 112:3).

I will be satisfied with long life, and God will show me His salvation (Ps. 91:16).

I dwell in the secret place of the Most High, and I abide under the shadow of the Almighty (Ps. 91:1).

No evil will befall me, and no plague shall come near my dwelling (Ps. 91:10).

My children are taught of the Lord, and great is their peace (Isa. 54:13).

I am strengthened with might by His Spirit in the inner man (Eph. 3:16).

I am rooted and grounded in love (Eph. 3:17).

I bless my natural enemies, and I overcome evil with good (Matt. 5:44).

PRAYERS FOR BLESSING AND FAVOR

Lord, bless me and keep me. Make Your face to shine upon me, and be gracious unto me. Lord, lift up Your countenance upon me and give me peace (Num. 6:24–26).

Make me as Ephraim and Manasseh (Gen. 48:20).

Let me be satisfied with favor and filled with Your blessing (Deut. 33:23).

Lord, command Your blessing upon my life.

Give me revelation, and let me be blessed (Matt. 16:17).

I am the seed of Abraham through Jesus Christ, and I receive the blessing of Abraham. Lord, in blessing, bless me, and in multiplying, multiply me as the stars of heaven and as the sand of the seashore.

Let Your showers of blessing be upon my life (Ezek. 34:26).

Turn every curse sent my way into a blessing (Neh. 13:2).

Let Your blessing make me rich (Prov. 10:22).

Let all nations call me blessed (Mal. 3:12).

Let all generations call me blessed (Luke 1:48).

I am a son of the blessed (Mark 14:61).

I live in the kingdom of the blessed (Mark 11:10).

My sins are forgiven, and I am blessed (Rom. 4:7).

Lord, You daily load me with benefits (Ps. 68:19).

I am chosen by God, and I am blessed (Ps. 65:4).

My seed is blessed (Ps. 37:26).

Let me inherit the land (Ps. 37:22).

I am a part of a holy nation, and I am blessed (Ps. 33:12).

Lord, bless my latter end more than my beginning (Job 42:12).

Lord, let Your presence bless my life (2 Sam. 6:11).

I drink the cup of blessing (1 Cor. 10:16).

Lord, bless me, and cause Your face to shine upon me,
that Your way may be known upon the earth and Your
saving health among all nations. Let my land yield increase,
and let the ends of the earth fear You (Ps. 67).

I know You favor me because my enemies
do not triumph over me (Ps. 41:11).

Lord, be favorable unto my land (Ps. 85:1).

Lord, grant me life and favor (Job 10:12).

In Your favor, Lord, make my mountain stand strong (Ps. 30:7).

Lord, I entreat Your favor (Ps. 45:12).

Let Your favor cause my horn to be exalted (Ps. 89:17).

Lord, this is my set time for favor (Ps. 102:13).

Remember me, O Lord, with the favor that You bring unto
Your children, and visit me with Your salvation (Ps. 106:4).

Lord, I entreat Your favor with my whole heart (Ps. 119:58).

Let Your favor be upon my life as a cloud
of the latter rain (Prov. 16:15).

Let Your beauty be upon my life, and let
me be well favored (Gen. 29:17).

I am highly favored (Luke 1:28).

Lord, let me receive extraordinary favor.

PRAYERS FOR REVELATION

You are a God that reveals secrets. Lord, reveal
Your secrets unto me (Dan. 2:28).

Reveal to me the secret and deep things (Dan. 2:22).

Let me understand things kept secret from the
foundation of the world (Matt. 13:35).

Let the seals be broken from Your Word (Dan. 12:9).

Let me understand and have revelation of
Your will and purpose for my life.

Give me the spirit of wisdom and revelation, and let the
eyes of my understanding be enlightened (Eph. 1:17).

Let me understand heavenly things (John 3:12).

Open my eyes to behold wondrous things
out of Your Word (Ps. 119:18).

Let me know and understand the mysteries
of the kingdom (Mark 4:11).

Let me speak to others by revelation (1 Cor. 14:6).

Reveal Your secrets to Your servants the prophets (Amos 3:7).

Let the hidden things be made manifest (Mark 4:22).

Hide Your truths from the wise and prudent,
and reveal them to babes (Matt. 11:25).

Let Your arm be revealed in my life (John 12:38).

Reveal the things that belong to me (Deut. 29:29).

Let Your Word be revealed unto me (1 Sam. 3:7).

Let Your glory be revealed in my life (Isa. 40:5).

Let Your righteousness be revealed in my life (Isa. 56:1).

Let me receive visions and revelations of the Lord (2 Cor. 12:1).

Let me receive an abundance of revelations (2 Cor. 12:7).

Let me be a good steward of Your revelations (1 Cor. 4:1).

Let me speak the mystery of Christ (Col. 4:3).

Let me receive and understand Your hidden wisdom (1 Cor. 2:7).

Hide not Your commandments from me (Ps. 119:19).

Let me speak the wisdom of God in a mystery (1 Cor. 2:7).

Let me make known the mystery of the gospel (Eph. 6:19).

Make known unto me the mystery of Your will (Eph. 1:9).

Open Your dark sayings upon the harp (Ps. 49:4).

Let me understand Your parables; the words of
the wise and their dark sayings (Prov. 1:6).

Lord, lighten my candle and enlighten my darkness (Ps. 18:28).

Make darkness light before me (Isa. 42:16).

Give me the treasures of darkness and hidden
riches in secret places (Isa. 45:3).

Let Your candle shine upon my head (Job 29:3).

My spirit is the candle of the Lord, searching all
the inward parts of the belly (Prov. 20:27).

Let me understand the deep things of God (1 Cor. 2:10).

Let me understand Your deep thoughts (Ps. 92:5).

Let my eyes be enlightened with Your Word (Ps. 19:8).

My eyes are blessed to see (Luke 10:23).

Let all spiritual cataracts and scales be
removed from my eyes (Acts 9:18).

Let me comprehend with all saints what is the breadth and
length and depth and height of Your love (Eph. 3:18).

Let my reins instruct me in the night season, and
let me awaken with revelation (Ps. 16:7).

PRAYERS CONCERNING THE HEAVENS

I am sitting in heavenly places in Christ, far above all
principality, power, might, and dominion (Eph. 1:3).

I take my position in the heavens and bind the principalities
and powers that operate against my life in the name of Jesus.

I break and rebuke every program in the heavens
that would operate against me through the sun,
the moon, the stars, and the constellations.

I bind and rebuke any ungodly forces operating against me
through Arcturus, Pleiades, Mazzaroth, and Orion (Job 38:31–32).

I bind and rebuke all moon deities and demons operating
through the moon in the name of Jesus (2 Kings 23:5).

I bind all sun deities and demons operating through
the sun in the name of Jesus (2 Kings 23:5).

I bind all deities and demons operating through the stars
and planets in the name of Jesus (2 Kings 23:5).

The sun shall not smite me by day nor the moon by night (Ps. 121:6).

The heavens were created to be a blessing to my life.

I receive the rain and blessing from heaven
upon my life in the name of Jesus.

I pray for angels to be released to war against any spirit in the heavens
assigned to block my prayers from being answered (Dan. 10:12–13).

I bind the prince of the power of the air
in the name of Jesus (Eph. 2:2).

I pray for the floodgates of heaven to be
opened over my life (Mal. 3:10).

I pray for an open heaven, and I bind any demonic
interference from the heavens in the name of Jesus.

Let the evil powers of heaven be shaken in
the name of Jesus (Matt. 24:29).

Let the heavens drop dew upon my life (Deut. 33:28).

Bow the heavens and come down, O Lord (Ps. 144:5).

Let the heavens be opened over my life,
and let me see visions (Ezek. 1:1).

Shake the heavens and fill my house with Your glory (Hag. 2:6–7).

Thunder in the heavens against the enemy, O Lord (Ps. 18:13).

Let the heavens drop at the presence of God (Ps. 68:8).

Let the heavens praise Thy wonders, O Lord (Ps. 89:5).

Show Your wonders in the heavens (Joel 2:30).

Ride upon the heavens and release Your voice, O Lord (Ps. 68:33).

Release Your manifold wisdom to the
powers in the heavens (Eph. 3:10).

PRAYERS FOR ENLARGEMENT AND INCREASE

Break off of my life any limitations and restrictions placed
on my life by any evil spirits in the name of Jesus.

I bind and cast out all python and constrictor
spirits in the name of Jesus.

Bless me indeed, and enlarge my coast. Let Your hand
be with me, and keep me from evil (1 Chron. 4:10).

Cast out my enemies, and enlarge my borders (Exod. 34:24).

Lord, You have promised to enlarge my borders (Deut. 12:20).

Enlarge my heart so I can run the way of
Your commandments (Ps. 119:32).

My mouth is enlarged over my enemies (1 Sam. 2:1).

Enlarge my steps so I can receive Your
wealth and prosperity (Isa. 60:5–9).

I receive deliverance and enlargement for my life (Esther 4:14).

The Lord shall increase me more and more,
me and my children (Ps. 115:14).

Let Your kingdom and government increase in my life (Isa. 9:7).

Let me increase in the knowledge of God (Col. 2:19).

O Lord, bless me and increase me (Isa. 51:2).

Let me increase exceedingly (Gen. 30:43).

Let me increase with the increase of God (Col. 2:19).

Let me increase and abound in love (1 Thess. 3:12).

Increase my greatness, and comfort me on every side (Ps. 71:21).

Let me increase in wisdom and stature (Luke 2:52).

Let me increase in strength and confound the adversaries (Acts 9:22).

Let Your grace and favor increase in my life.

Let the years of my life be increased (Prov. 9:11).

Let the Word of God increase in my life (Acts 6:7).

Bless me in all my increase (Deut. 14:22).

Let my giving and tithes increase (Deut. 14:22).

Let my latter end greatly increase (Job 8:7).

Let me grow in grace and in the knowledge
of Jesus Christ (2 Pet. 3:18).

I will flourish like a palm tree and grow like
a cedar in Lebanon (Ps. 92:12).

Let my faith grow exceedingly (2 Thess. 1:3).

The breaker is gone up before me and broken through
every limitation and barrier of the enemy (Mic. 2:13).

Lord, You are the God of the breakthrough. You have
broken forth against my enemies (2 Sam. 5:20).

My branches run over every wall erected by the enemy (Gen. 49:22).

I can run through a troop and leap over a wall (Ps. 18:29).

Let my line go through all the earth, and my
words to the end of the world (Ps. 19:4).

I am a joint heir with Jesus Christ. Give me the
heathen for my inheritance and the uttermost part
of the earth for my possession (Ps. 2:8).

RENUNCIATIONS

I renounce all lust, perversion, immorality, uncleanness,
impurity, and sexual sin in the name of Jesus.

I renounce all witchcraft, sorcery, divination, and
occult involvement in the name of Jesus.

I renounce all ungodly soul ties and immoral
relationships in the name of Jesus.

I renounce all hatred, anger, resentment, revenge, retaliation,
unforgiveness, and bitterness in the name of Jesus.

I forgive any person who has ever hurt me, disappointed me,
abandoned me, mistreated me, or rejected me in the name of Jesus.

I renounce all addiction to drugs, alcohol, or any legal or
illegal substance that has bound me in the name of Jesus.

I renounce all pride, haughtiness, arrogance, vanity, ego,
disobedience, and rebellion in the name of Jesus.

I renounce all envy, jealousy, and covetousness in the name of Jesus.

I renounce all fear, unbelief, and doubt in the name of Jesus.

I renounce all selfishness, self-will, self-pity, self-rejection,
self-hatred, and self-promotion in the name of Jesus.

I renounce all ungodly thought patterns and
belief systems in the name of Jesus.

I renounce all ungodly covenants, oaths, and vows made
by myself or my ancestors in the name of Jesus.

PRAYERS IN CHRIST

I am called in Christ (Rom. 1:6).

I have redemption in Christ (Rom. 3:24).

I reign in life by Christ (Rom. 5:17).

I am alive unto God through Christ (Rom. 6:11).

I have eternal life through Christ (Rom. 6:23).

I am a joint heir with Christ (Rom. 8:17).

I am sanctified in Christ (1 Cor. 1:2).

My body is a member of Christ (1 Cor. 6:15).

I have victory through Christ (1 Cor. 15:57).

I triumph in Christ (2 Cor. 2:14).

I am a new creature in Christ (2 Cor. 5:17).

I am the righteousness of God in Christ (2 Cor. 5:21).

I have liberty in Christ (Gal. 2:4).

I am crucified with Christ (Gal. 2:20).

I have put on Christ (Gal. 3:27).

I am an heir of God through Christ (Gal. 4:7).

I have been blessed with spiritual blessings in
heavenly places in Christ (Eph. 1:3).

I have been chosen in Christ before the foundation of the world,
that I should be holy and without blame before Him (Eph. 1:4).

I have obtained an inheritance in Christ (Eph. 1:11).

I have been quickened with Christ (Eph. 2:5).

I am sitting in heavenly places in Christ (Eph. 2:6).

I have been created in Christ unto good works (Eph. 2:10).

I have boldness and access in Christ (Eph. 3:12).

I rejoice in Christ (Phil. 3:3).

I press toward the mark of the high calling
of God in Christ (Phil. 3:14).

I can do all things through Christ who strengthens me (Phil. 4:13).

God supplies all my needs through Christ (Phil. 4:19).

Christ in me is the hope of glory (Col. 1:27).

I am complete in Christ (Col. 2:10).

I am dead with Christ (Col. 2:20).

I am risen with Christ (Col. 3:1).

My life is hidden with Christ in God (Col. 3:3).

Christ is my life (Col. 3:4).

I have the mind of Christ (1 Cor. 2:16).

I am a partaker of Christ (Heb. 3:14).

I am preserved in Christ (Jude 1:1).

KINGDOM PRAYERS AND DECREES

Your kingdom come; Your will be done (Matt. 6:10).

Let Your kingdom advance and be established through
preaching, teaching, and healing (Matt. 4:23).

Let the gates of my life and city be opened for
the King of glory to come in (Ps. 24:7).

Lord, You reign. You are clothed with majesty and strength. Your
throne is established of old. You are from everlasting (Ps. 93:1–2).

Lord, You are a great king above all gods (Ps. 95:3).

Let the heathen hear that the Lord reigns (Ps. 96:10).

Lord, You reign. Let the people tremble;
let the earth be moved (Ps. 99:1).

Lord, You have prepared Your throne in the heavens,
and Your kingdom rules over all (Ps. 103:19).

Let men bless the Lord in all places of His dominion (Ps. 103:22).

Your kingdom is an everlasting kingdom, and Your dominion
endures throughout all generations (Ps. 145:13).

Let men speak of the glory of Your kingdom
and talk of Your power (Ps. 145:11).

Let men know Your mighty acts and the glorious
majesty of Your kingdom (Ps. 145:12).

Let your kingdom come through deliverance (Matt. 12:22).

Let the gospel of the kingdom be preached in my
region with signs and wonders following.

Father, I receive the kingdom because it is Your
good pleasure to give it to me (Luke 12:32).

Let the righteousness, peace, and joy of the kingdom
be established in my life (Rom. 14:17).

Let the kingdoms of this world become the kingdoms
of our Lord and of His Christ (Rev. 11:15).

Let the saints possess the kingdom (Dan. 7:22).

Overthrow the thrones of wicked kingdoms (Hag. 2:22).

Preserve me unto Your heavenly kingdom (2 Tim. 4:18).

Let the scepter of Your kingdom be released (Heb. 1:8).

I seek first the kingdom of God and His righteousness,
and all things are added unto me (Matt. 6:33).

Break in pieces and consume every demonic
kingdom that resists your dominion (Ps. 72:8).

Let all dominions serve and obey You, O Lord (Dan. 7:27).

PRAYERS RELEASING THE FIRE OF GOD

Your throne, O Lord, is like a fiery flame (Dan. 7:9).

You are the God that answers by fire (1 Kings 18:24).

A fire goes before You, O Lord, and burns up Your enemies (Ps. 97:3).

Lord, release Your fire and burn up the works of darkness.

Baptize me with the Holy Ghost and fire (Luke 3:16).

Let Your fire be in my hands to heal the sick and cast out devils.

Let Your fire burn in my eyes, my heart,
my belly, my mouth, and my feet.

Let Your fire be in my tongue to preach and prophesy.

I receive tongues of fire.

Let Your Word be preached with fire (Jer. 23:29).

Make me a minister of fire (Heb. 1:7).

Deliver me with Your fire (Ps. 18:13).

Let Your fire protect me and cover me (Exod. 14:24).

I release the fire of God to burn up the idols of the land (Deut. 7:5).

Let the works of witchcraft and occultism
be burned in Your fire (Acts 19:19).

Purify my life with Your fire (Mal. 3:2).

Let Your fire be released in Zion (Isa. 31:9).

Let the spirits of lust and perversion be
destroyed with Your fire (Gen. 19:24).

Release the spirit of burning to burn up the
works of darkness (Ps. 140:10).

Let Your flame burn up wicked spirits (Ps. 106:18).

Let Your glory kindle a burning like the burning of a fire (Isa. 10:16).

Cause Your glorious voice to be heard. Show lightning down Your arm with a flame of devouring fire, with scattering, tempest, and hailstones (Isa. 30:30).

Let Babylon be as stubble, and let Your fire burn them. Let them not be able to deliver themselves from the power of the flame (Isa. 47:14).

Lord, come and rebuke Your enemies with flames of fire (Isa. 66:15).

Let all flesh see Your fire released (Ezek. 20:48).

Create upon Zion a flaming fire by night (Isa. 4:5).

Let the fire of Your presence be released in my life (Ps. 97:5).

Let demons be exposed and cast out with Your fire (Acts 28:3).

Release Your hot thunderbolts against the enemy (Ps. 78:48).

Cast forth lightning, and scatter the enemy (Ps. 144:6).

Let Your light be for a fire, and Your Holy One for a flame to burn the briers and thorns in my life (Isa. 10:17).

PRAYERS TO COMMAND THE MORNING, THE DAY, AND THE NIGHT

I command the morning to take hold of the ends of the earth and shake the wicked out of it (Job 38:12).

I will have dominion over the devil in the morning (Ps. 49:14).

Lord, make the outgoings of the morning to rejoice (Ps. 65:8).

I receive Your lovingkindness every morning (Ps. 143:8).

Release the beauty of Your holiness from the womb of the morning (Ps. 110:3).

Let Your light break forth in my life as the morning (Ps. 58:8).

Let Your judgments come upon the enemy morning by morning (Isa. 28:19).

Lord, Your going forth is prepared as the morning, and we pray that You will come as the rain, the latter and former rain upon the earth (Hos. 6:3).

Lord, You visit me every morning (Job 7:18).

Lord, You awaken me morning by morning. You waken my ear to hear as the learned (Isa. 50:4).

I will not be afraid of the arrow that flies by day or the terror that comes at night (Ps. 91:5).

Lord, show forth Your salvation in my life from day to day (Ps. 96:2).

I bind the screech owl in the name of Jesus (Isa. 34:14).

I bind any attack upon my life at night.

I take authority over every demon that is released against me and my family at night.

Let the evening tide trouble the enemies that would attack my life in the name of Jesus (Isa. 17:12–14).

I bind and rebuke every spirit that would creep against me at night (Ps. 104:20).

I bind and rebuke the pestilence that walks in darkness (Ps. 91:6).

I will rest at night because the Lord gives me sleep.

Let Your angels guard and protect me at night.

Lord, give me deliverance in the night season (Acts 12:6–7).

Lord, let my reins instruct me in the night season (Ps. 16:7).

Your song shall be with me in the night (Ps. 42:8).

I will meditate upon You in the night watches (Ps. 63:6).

I receive Your knowledge in the night (Ps. 19:2).

I receive Your faithfulness every night (Ps. 92:2).

I bind and rebuke every vampire spirit in the name of Jesus (Lev. 11:19).

I bind and rebuke all incubus and succubus spirits that would attack at night in the name of Jesus.

I bind and take authority over all nightmares and demonic dreams at night in the name of Jesus.

I am set in my ward whole nights (Isa. 21:8).

RELEASING THE SWORD OF THE LORD

I release the sword of the Lord against the powers of hell in the name of Jesus (Judg. 7:18).

I will whet my glittering sword and render Your vengeance against the enemy (Deut. 32:41).

Gird Your sword upon Your thigh, and ride prosperously through the earth (Ps. 45:3).

Let your enemies fall by the sword (Ps. 63:10).

Let the Assyrian fall with the sword (Isa. 31:8).

I release the sword of the Lord against leviathan (Isa. 27:1).

Send Your angels with flaming swords to fight my battles in the heavens.

I release the two-edged sword to execute judgments written (Ps. 149:6).

Release the sword out of Your mouth against the enemy (Rev. 19:15).

RELEASING THE ARROWS OF THE LORD

I release the arrow of the Lord's deliverance in my life (2 Kings 13:17).

I release Your sharp arrows into the heart of the King's enemies (Ps. 45:5).

Ordain and release Your arrows against my persecutors (Ps. 7:13).

Send out Your arrows, and scatter the enemy (Ps. 18:14).

Make my enemies turn their back with Your arrows upon Your strings (Ps. 21:12).

Shoot out Your arrows, and destroy them (Ps. 144:6).

Send Your arrows abroad (Ps. 77:17).

Send out arrows of light into the kingdom of darkness (Hab. 3:11).

Heap mischief upon them, and spend Your arrows upon them (Deut. 32:23).

Shoot Your arrows upon them, and let them be wounded suddenly (Ps. 64:7).

Let Your arrow go forth as lightning against the enemy (Zech. 9:14).

Break their bones, and pierce them through with Your arrows (Num. 24:8).

Shoot at Your enemies with Your arrows (Ps. 64:7).

Set Your mark upon my enemies for Your arrows (Lam. 3:12).

Make Your arrows bright, and release Your vengeance upon my enemies (Jer. 51:11).

BREAKING CURSES AND CASTING OUT GENERATIONAL SPIRITS

I am redeemed from the curse of the law (Gal. 3:13).

I break all generational curses of pride, lust, perversion, rebellion, witchcraft, idolatry, poverty, rejection, fear, confusion, addiction, death, and destruction in the name of Jesus.

I command all generational spirits that came into my life during conception, in the womb, in the birth canal, and through the umbilical cord to come out in the name of Jesus.

I break all spoken curses and negative words that I have spoken over my life in the name of Jesus.

I break all spoken curses and negative words spoken over my life by others, including those in authority, in the name of Jesus.

I command all ancestral spirits of freemasonry, idolatry, witchcraft, false religion, polygamy, lust, and perversion to come out of my life in the name of Jesus.

I command all hereditary spirits of lust, rejection, fear, sickness, infirmity, disease, anger, hatred, confusion, failure, and poverty to come out of my life in the name of Jesus.

I break the legal rights of all generational spirits operating behind a curse in the name of Jesus. You have no legal right to operate in my life.

I bind and rebuke all familiar spirits and spirit guides that would try to operate in my life from my ancestors in the name of Jesus.

I renounce all false beliefs and philosophies inherited by my ancestors in the name of Jesus.

I break all curses on my finances from any ancestors that cheated or mishandled money in the name of Jesus.

I break all curses of sickness and disease and command all inherited sickness to leave my body in the name of Jesus.

Through Jesus, my family is blessed (Gen. 12:3).

I renounce all pride inherited from my ancestors in the name of Jesus.

I break all oaths, vows, and pacts made with the devil by my ancestors in the name of Jesus.

I break all curses by agents of Satan spoken against my life in secret in the name of Jesus (Ps. 10:7).

I break all written curses that would affect my life in the name of Jesus (2 Chron. 34:24).

I break every time-released curse that would activate in my life as I grow older in the name of Jesus.

I break every curse Balaam hired against my
life in the name of Jesus (Neh. 13:2).

Lord, turn every curse spoken against my
life into a blessing (Neh. 13:2).

I break all generational rebellion that would cause
me to resist the Holy Spirit (Acts 7:51).

I break all curses of death spoken by people in authority
in my nation over my nation in the name of Jesus.

I break curses of death spoken against America by
people from other nations in the name of Jesus.

ANNULLING UNGODLY COVENANTS

I break and disannul all ungodly covenants, oaths, and
pledges I have made with my lips in the name of Jesus.

I renounce and break all ungodly oaths made by my
ancestors to idols, demons, false religions, or ungodly
organizations in the name of Jesus (Matt. 5:33).

I break and disannul all covenants with death and
hell made by my ancestors in the name of Jesus.

I break and disannul all ungodly covenants made with idols or
demons by my ancestors in the name of Jesus (Exod. 23:32).

I break and disannul all blood covenants made through
sacrifice that would affect my life in the name of Jesus.

I command all demons that claim any legal right to my life
through covenants to come out in the name of Jesus.

I break and disannul any covenant made with false
gods and demons through the occult involvement
and witchcraft in the name of Jesus.

I break and disannul all spirit marriages that would cause incubus
and succubus demons to attack my life in the name of Jesus.

I break and disannul any marriage to any demon
that would affect my life in the name of Jesus.

I break all agreements with hell in the name of Jesus (Isa. 28:18).

I have a covenant with God through the blood of Jesus
Christ. I am joined to the Lord, and I am one spirit
with Him. I break all ungodly covenants and renew my
covenant to God through the body and blood of Jesus.

I divorce myself from any demon that would claim my life
through any ancestral covenants in the name of Jesus.

I bind and cast out any family demon that would follow my
life through ancestral covenants in the name of Jesus.

SECTION 2

PREPARING to ENGAGE the ENEMY

WHAT MAKES A PERSON SUCCESSFUL IN SPIRITUAL warfare? Some of the qualifications include:

- *Endurance* (2 Tim. 2:3)—the ability to endure and withstand hardship, adversity, or stress. We are to endure hardness as a good soldier of Jesus Christ.

- *Hatred* (Ps. 139:22)—extreme dislike or antipathy, loathing. In spiritual warfare, we must have a hatred of evil and evil spirits.

- *Knowledge* (2 Cor. 2:11)—we are not to be ignorant of Satan's devices.

- *Persistence* (Ps. 18:37)—the ability to go on resolutely or stubbornly in spite of oppression. We must be persistent in dealing with the enemy.

- *Separation* (2 Tim. 2:14)—to get or keep apart. No man who wars entangles himself with the affairs of this life.

God uses ordinary people to accomplish His purposes. Our ability comes through grace. Every believer is sitting in heavenly places in Christ. Your position in Christ is high above all principality and power. You must see who you are *in Christ*. You can do all things through Christ.

It is important to know your authority and engage the enemy in faith. There is no need to fear. Demons are subject to the authority of the believer. Jesus gives us power to tread on serpents and scorpions (Luke 10:19). He promised that nothing will by any means harm us.

Joshua was told to engage the enemy (Deut. 2:24). You will see great victories through engagement. *To engage* means "to bring troops into conflict." There are some believers who fear engagement. They are afraid of backlash. Jesus sent His disciples out to engage the enemy. They were told to heal the sick and cast out devils.

Two important revelations every believer needs are an understanding of *power* and an understanding of *authority*. *Power* is the Greek word *dunamis*. *Authority* is the Greek word *exousia*. Authority is the legal right to use power. We have been given authority to use the power supplied by the Holy Spirit.

Authority and power must be used. You use them by faith. This is not based on feeling but on faith. It is based on the Word of God. Faith comes by hearing the Word of God. It is important for believers to attend churches that teach on power and authority. It is important to read and study on these subjects. Revelation in these areas will give confidence to pray these prayers.

We have been given the legal right to use the name of Jesus. The name of Jesus is above every name. Authority in the name of Jesus is recognized by the spirit realm. We cast out demons in that name. We bind the works of darkness in that name. We teach and preach in that name.

We receive power through the Holy Spirit (Acts 1:8). God is able to do exceeding abundantly according to the power that operates in us. Jesus cast out demons through the power of the Holy Spirit (Matt. 12:28). We combine the power of the Holy Spirit with the authority of the name of Jesus to rout the enemy. We do not engage the enemy in our own power and authority. We engage the enemy through the power of the Holy Spirit and in the authority of the name of Jesus.

Demons recognize power and authority. They recognize believers who operate in power and authority. The more you exercise power and authority, the more you will develop in these areas. It is important to start. The prayers in this book will help you get started.

It is also important to make sure your sins are forgiven when engaging the enemy. If we confess our sins, He is faithful and just to forgive us, and to cleanse us from all unrighteousness (1 John 1:9). Do not engage the enemy with unconfessed sin in your life. There is power in the blood of Jesus. His blood cleanses us from all sin. Give no place to the devil. You must operate in righteousness.

We are made righteous through faith. We are the righteousness of God in Christ (2 Cor. 5:21). Many believers suffer from feelings of inferiority and low self-esteem because they do not understand righteousness. Righteousness gives us confidence. Righteousness gives us boldness. Righteousness is the scepter of the kingdom (Heb. 1:8). The righteous are as bold as a lion (Prov. 28:1).

God covers our heads in the day of battle (Ps. 140:7). A covering is protection. Covering is based on subjection to God, His Word, and the Holy Spirit. Humility and submission are important characteristics of believers who engage in spiritual warfare. These prayers are not for people who are rebellious. It is important to be submitted to proper biblical authority. This includes being submitted to godly leaders who watch for your soul.

Prayers for Divine Safety and Protection

I cover myself, my family, and my possessions with the blood of Jesus.

Let the fire of God surround and protect
my life from all destruction.

Let the angel of the Lord encamp around
me and protect me (Ps. 34:7).

Let Your glory be my covering and protect my back.

Hold me up, and I will be safe (Ps. 119:117).

The name of Jesus is a strong tower. I run
into it, and I am safe (Prov. 18:10).

Lord, You make me to dwell in safety (Ps. 4:8).

Set me in safety from them who puff at me (Ps. 12:5).

Let me dwell in my land safely (Lev. 26:5).

Lead me safely, and I will not fear. Let the sea
overwhelm my enemies (Ps. 78:53).

Let me lie down and rest in safety (Job 11:18; Isa. 14:30).

I will dwell in safety; nothing
shall make me afraid (Ezek. 34:28).

Keep me as the apple of Your eye, and hide me
under the shadow of Your wings (Ps. 17:8).

I will trust in the covert of Your wings (Ps. 61:4).

In the shadow of Your wings will I trust (Ps. 57:1).

Be my covert from the storm and the rain (Isa. 4:6).

Be my covert from the wind and the tempest (Isa. 32:2).

Cover my head in the day of battle (Ps. 140:7).

Cover me with the shadow of Your hand (Isa. 51:16).

Cover me with Your feathers (Ps. 91:4).

Be my defense and refuge (Ps. 59:16).

Defend and deliver me (Isa. 31:5).

Let Your glory be my defense (Isa. 4:5).

Defend me from those who rise up against me (Ps. 59:1).

Lord, You are my shield and my hiding place (Ps. 119:114).

Lord, surround me with Your shield of protection (Ps. 5:12).

Bring them down, O Lord, my shield (Ps. 59:11).

Let Your truth be my shield (Ps. 91:4).

Lord, You are my sun and shield (Ps. 84:11).

Lord, You are my shield and exceeding great reward (Gen. 15:1).

I will not be afraid of ten thousand that have set themselves against me, because You are a shield for me (Ps. 3:1–6).

You are a strong tower from the enemy (Ps. 61:3).

PRAYERS TO RELEASE THE ARM OF THE LORD

No one has an arm like You, Lord, full of power and might (Job 40:9).

Lord, You have a mighty arm. Your hand is strong, and Your right hand is high (Ps. 89:13).

Stretch out Your arm and deliver me, and rid me out of all bondage (Exod. 6:6).

Let fear and dread fall upon the enemy by the greatness of Your arm until I pass over (Exod. 15:16).

Favor me, and let Your right arm bring me into my possession (Ps. 44:3).

Break Rahab in pieces, and scatter Your enemies with Your strong arm (Ps. 89:10).

Let Your hand establish me, and let Your arm strengthen me (Ps. 89:21).

Your right hand and Your holy arm give me victory (Ps. 98:1).

Show lightning down Your arm against my enemies (Isa. 30:30).

I trust in Your arm for my salvation (Isa. 51:5).

Awake, awake, and put on strength, O arm of the Lord. Awake as in the ancient days. Cut Rahab, and wound the dragon (Isa. 51:9).

Make bare Your holy arm in the sight of all nations, and let all flesh see Your salvation (Isa. 52:10).

Show strength with Your arm, and scatter the proud (Luke 1:51).

Reveal Your arm unto me, that I might know Your strength and power.

Let the power in Your hands be released in my life (Hab. 3:4).

RELEASING THE POWER OF GOD

Lord, release Your glorious power against the enemy (Exod. 15:6).

Let power and might be released from Your hand (1 Chron. 29:12).

Scatter the enemy by Your power (Ps. 59:11).

Rule over Your enemies through Your power (Ps. 66:7).

Let the power of Your anger be released against the powers of darkness (Ps. 90:11).

I release the power and authority of the Lord against all demons I encounter in the name of Jesus (Matt. 10:1).

I am delivered from the power of Satan unto God (Acts 26:18).

Divide the sea, and destroy marine spirits through Your power (Job 26:12).

I am strong in the Lord and in the power of His might (Eph. 6:10).

Cause the powers of darkness to submit to Your power.

Display Your awesome power that men will believe.

Release Your power in healing and deliverance (Luke 5:17).

Release Your powerful voice (Ps. 29:4).

Let me be amazed at Your power (Luke 9:43).

Let great power be released through Your apostles (Acts 4:33).

Let signs, wonders, and miracles be released through
the power of the Holy Spirit (Rom. 15:19).

Let me preach and teach with demonstration
of the Spirit and power (1 Cor. 2:4).

Let Your power work in me (Eph. 3:20).

Release Your powerful angels on my behalf to fight
my battles in the heavens (2 Pet. 2:11; Rev. 18:1).

Release the power of Elijah through Your prophets (Luke 1:17).

Let me be willing in the day of Your power (Ps. 110:3).

RELEASING THE POWER OF THE BLOOD

I cover my mind and thoughts with the blood of Jesus.

I cover my doorpost and possessions with
the blood of Jesus (Exod. 12:13).

I overcome the devil through the blood of Jesus (Rev. 12:11).

I sprinkle the blood of Jesus and receive
multiplied grace and peace (1 Pet. 1:2).

I am made perfect through the blood of the
everlasting covenant (Heb. 13:20–21).

I have boldness to enter into the presence of
God through the blood (Heb. 10:19).

My conscience is purged from dead works to serve the
living God through the blood of Jesus (Heb. 9:14).

I eat the body of Jesus and drink His blood (John 6:54).

I have redemption through the blood of Jesus, and I am redeemed from the power of evil (Eph. 1:7).

I rebuke all spirits of torment and fear because I have peace through the blood of Jesus (Col. 1:20).

I receive the benefits of the new covenant through the blood of Jesus (Matt. 26:28).

I receive healing and health through the blood of Jesus.

I receive abundance and prosperity through the blood of Jesus.

I receive deliverance through the blood of Jesus.

I receive the fullness of the Holy Spirit and the anointing through the blood of Jesus.

The blood of Jesus bears witness to my deliverance and salvation (1 John 5:8).

The blood of Jesus cleanses me from all sin (1 John 1:7).

Jesus resisted unto blood, and His blood gives me victory (Heb. 12:4).

I rebuke and cast out all spirits of guilt, shame, and condemnation through the blood of Jesus.

I break the power of sin and iniquity in my life through the blood of Jesus (Heb. 10:17).

My heart is sprinkled and purified by the blood of Jesus from an evil conscience (Heb. 10:22).

I rebuke Satan, the accuser of the brethren, through the blood of Jesus (Rev. 12:10).

I command all my accusers to depart through the blood of Jesus (John 8:10).

I rebuke and cast out all spirits of slander and accusation through the blood of Jesus (Matt. 12:10).

I release the voice of the blood against demons and evil spirits that would accuse and condemn me (Heb. 12:24).

WARFARE PRAYERS

Lord, teach my hands to war and my fingers to fight (Ps. 144:1).

Lord, I am Your End Times warrior. Use me as Your weapon against the enemy (2 Chron. 11:1).

The weapons of my warfare are not carnal but mighty through You to the pulling down of strongholds (2 Cor. 10:4).

Satan, you have lost the war in heaven (Rev. 12:7).

Let all the enemies that make war with the Lamb be destroyed (Rev. 17:14).

I do not war after the flesh but after the spirit (2 Cor. 10:3).

Lord, thunder upon the enemy; release Your voice; hail stones and coals of fire (Ps. 18:13).

Send out Your arrows, and scatter them. Shoot out Your light and discomfit them (Ps. 18:14).

Deliver me from my strong enemy, from them that are too strong for me (Ps. 18:17).

Deliver me, and bring me into a large place (Ps. 18:19).

I am your battle-ax and weapon of war (Jer. 51:20).

You have given me the necks of my enemies, and I will destroy them in the name of Jesus (Ps. 18:40).

I am Your anointed, and You give me great deliverance (Ps. 18:50).

I will beat them small as the dust and cast them out as mire in the streets (Ps. 18:42).

I have pursued my enemies and overtaken them. I did not turn until they were consumed (Ps. 18:37).

I have wounded them, and they are not able to rise.
They have fallen under my feet (Ps. 18:38).

I tread upon the lion and adder. The young lion
and dragon I trample underfoot (Ps. 91:13).

I tread upon serpents and scorpions and over all the power of the
enemy, and nothing shall by any means hurt me (Luke 10:19).

I tread down the wicked; they are ashes under my feet (Mal. 4:3).

I will arise and thresh and beat the enemy into pieces (Mic. 4:13).

I rebuke every wild boar of the field in the name of Jesus (Ps. 80:13).

I rebuke every spirit that creeps forth from the forest (Ps. 104:20).

I rebuke every beast of the forest that comes to devour (Isa. 56:9).

I rebuke every lion of the forest that comes to slay (Jer. 5:6).

I close the door to every demonic rat that would attempt
to come into my life in the name of Jesus (Isa. 66:17).

I bind and cast out every thief that would try to steal
my finances in the name of Jesus (John 10:10).

I bind and cast out any spirit that would try
to steal my joy in the name of Jesus.

I bind, expose, and cast out any demon that would try by
stealth (undetected) to come into my life (2 Sam. 19:3).

Lord, cleanse my temple and drive out any
thief from my life (John 2:14–15).

Lord, lift up a standard against any flood the enemy
would try to bring into my life (Isa. 59:19).

I bind and cast out all familiar spirits that would try to
operate in my life in the name of Jesus (Isa. 8:19).

I bind and rebuke any demon that would try to block
my way in the name of Jesus (Matt. 8:28).

I remove all leaven of malice and wickedness
from my life (1 Cor. 5:8).

I rebuke and cast out any froglike spirit from
my life in the name of Jesus (Rev. 16:13).

I bind and rebuke devils in high places in
the name of Jesus (2 Chron. 11:15).

I break off any fellowship with devils through sin, the
flesh, or sacrifice in the name of Jesus (1 Cor. 10:20).

I command all devils to leave my children
in the name of Jesus (Mark 7:29).

Lord, expose any human devils in my life
in the name of Jesus (John 6:70).

Lord, expose any children of the devil that would
try to come into the church (Acts 13:10).

Let every spirit hiding from me be exposed
in the name of Jesus (Josh. 10:16).

Let every hidden snare for my feet be exposed (Jer. 18:22).

I stand against and rebuke every wile of the devil (Eph. 6:11).

I release myself from any snare of the devil
in the name of Jesus (2 Tim. 2:26).

I will not come into the condemnation of the devil (1 Tim. 3:6).

Lord, let no doctrine of the devil be
established in my life (1 Tim. 4:1).

I nullify the power of any sacrifice made to devils in my
city, region, or nation in the name of Jesus (Lev. 17:7).

I bind and rebuke Molech and any spirit that has
been assigned to abort my destiny (Lev. 18:21).

Give me strength to bring forth my destiny (Isa. 66:9).

I overcome every antichrist spirit because greater is He that is in me than he that is in the world (1 John 4:4–5).

I loose myself from every spirit of error in the name of Jesus (1 John 4:6).

Lord, let me not operate in the wrong spirit (Luke 9:55).

I loose myself from every spirit of whoredom in the name of Jesus (Hos. 4:12).

Let me have and walk in an excellent spirit (Dan. 6:3).

I will take heed to my spirit at all times (Mal. 2:15).

I bind and cast out any spirit that would try to tear apart my life in any manner in the name of Jesus (Mark 9:20).

Lord, stir up my spirit to do Your will (Hag. 1:14).

I bind and cast out any demon of slumber from my life in the name of Jesus (Rom. 11:8).

I bind and cast out all demons of fear and timidity in the name of Jesus (2 Tim. 1:7).

I bind and cast out all seducing spirits that would come my way in the name of Jesus (1 Tim. 4:1).

I bind and rebuke the angel of light in the name of Jesus (2 Cor. 11:14).

I reject all false apostolic ministries in the name of Jesus (2 Cor. 11:13).

I reject all false prophetic ministries in the name of Jesus (Matt. 7:15).

I reject all false teaching ministries in the name of Jesus (2 Pet. 2:1).

Expose all false brethren to me (2 Cor. 11:26).

I reject the mouth of vanity and the right hand of falsehood (Ps. 144:8).

I reject every false vision and every false prophetic word released into my life (Jer. 14:14).

I bind Satan, the deceiver, from releasing any deception into my life (Rev. 12:9).

I bind and cast out all spirits of self-deception in the name of Jesus (1 Cor. 3:18).

I bind and cast out any spirit of sorcery that would deceive me in the name of Jesus (Rev. 18:23).

Lord, let no man deceive me (Matt. 24:4).

I bind and rebuke any bewitchment that would keep me from obeying the truth (Gal. 3:1).

I pray for utterance and boldness to make known the mystery of the gospel (Eph. 6:19).

Deliver me out of the hand of wicked and unreasonable men (2 Thess. 3:2).

Evil spirits leave my life as I hear and speak the Word (Matt. 8:16).

I rebuke, still, and cast out the avenger (Ps. 8:2).

I bind and cast out any creeping spirit that would attempt to creep into my life (Ezek. 8:10).

Let the hammer of the wicked be broken (Jer. 50:23).

I renounce all earthly, sensual, and demonic wisdom (James 3:15).

I cast out devils, and I will be perfected (Luke 13:32).

Let every Pharaoh that would pursue my life be drowned in the sea (Exod. 15:4).

I rebuke every demonic bee that would surround me in the name of Jesus (Ps. 118:12).

I bind and cast out any spirit of Absalom that would try to steal my heart from God's ordained leadership (2 Sam. 15:6).

I will sleep well. I will not be kept awake by any
spirit of restlessness or insomnia (Ps. 3:5).

I laugh at the enemy through the Holy Spirit (Ps. 2:4).

I cut the cords of the wicked from my life (Ps. 129:4).

Let every cord the enemy tries to put around my
life be like burning flax (Judg. 15:14).

I break down every wall of Jericho (Josh. 6:5).

Lord, cleanse my life from secret faults (Ps. 19:12).

Lord, let Your secret be upon my tabernacle (Job 29:4).

Lead me and guide me for Your name's sake (Ps. 31:3).

Guide me continually (Isa. 58:11).

Guide me into all truth (John 16:13).

Guide me with Your eye (Ps. 32:8).

Let me guide my affairs with discretion (Ps. 112:5).

Guide me by the skillfulness of Your hands (Ps. 78:72).

Lead me in a plain path because of my enemies (Ps. 27:11).

Lead me not into temptation, but deliver me from evil (Matt. 6:13).

Lead me, and make Your way straight before my eyes (Ps. 5:8).

Make the crooked places straight and the rough
places smooth before me (Isa. 40:4).

Send out Your light and truth, and let them lead me (Ps. 43:3).

Make darkness light before me and crooked
things straight (Isa. 42:16).

Teach me to do your will, and lead me into
the land of uprightness (Ps. 143:10).

I put on the garment of praise for the spirit of heaviness (Isa. 61:3).

Clothe me with the garment of salvation (Isa. 61:10).

I put on my beautiful garments (Isa. 52:1).

Let my garments always be white (Eccles. 9:8).

Let me be clothed with humility (1 Pet. 5:5).

Cover me with the robe of righteousness (Isa. 61:10).

Let my clothes be full of Your virtue (Mark 5:30).

Let a mantle of power rest upon my life (2 Kings 2:8).

Lord, give me wisdom in every area where I lack (James 1:5).

Prayers to Root Out

Let every plant that my Father has not planted
be rooted out in the name of Jesus.

I lay the ax to the root of every evil tree in my life.

Let every ungodly generational taproot be cut and
pulled out of my bloodline in the name of Jesus.

Let the roots of wickedness be as rottenness.

I speak to every evil tree to be uprooted
and cast into the sea (Luke 17:6).

Let Your holy fire burn up every ungodly
root in the name of Jesus (Mal. 4:1).

Let the confidence of the enemy be rooted out (Job 18:14).

Let every root of bitterness be cut from my life (Heb. 12:15).

Let the prophetic word be released to root
out evil kingdoms (Jer. 1:10).

Let any evil person planted in my church be
rooted out in the name of Jesus.

Let any sickness rooted in my body be
plucked up in the name of Jesus.

Let all false ministries that have rooted
themselves in my city be plucked up.

Let every bramble and nettle be plucked up
from my life in the name of Jesus.

Let all thorns be burned out of my life in
the name of Jesus (Isa. 10:17).

Let all spirits rooted in rejection come out in the name of Jesus.

Let all spirits rooted in pride come out in the name of Jesus.

Let all spirits rooted in rebellion come out in the name of Jesus.

Let all spirits rooted in fear come out in the name of Jesus.

Let all spirits rooted in lust and sexual sin
come out in the name of Jesus.

Let all spirits rooted in curses come out in the name of Jesus.

Let all spirits rooted in witchcraft come out in the name of Jesus.

Let all spirits rooted in any part of my body and
organs come out in the name of Jesus.

PRAYERS AGAINST SATAN (THE DEVIL)

Satan, the Lord rebuke thee (Zech. 3:2).

Get thee hence, Satan, for it is written (Matt. 4:10).

Get behind me, Satan, for it is written (Luke 4:8).

I beheld Satan as lightning fall from heaven (Luke 10:18).

I loose myself from every bond of Satan in
the name of Jesus (Luke 13:16).

Lord, bruise Satan under my feet (Rom. 16:20).

I bind and rebuke all hindering spirits of Satan
in the name of Jesus (1 Thess. 2:18).

I renounce all ungodly anger, and I give
no place to the devil (Eph. 4:27).

I pray to overcome any sifting that Satan would
try to bring into my life (Luke 22:31).

I am delivered from the power of Satan unto God (Acts 26:18).

I bind the thief from stealing, killing, or
destroying in my life (John 10:10).

Lord, remove Satan's seat from my region,
city, and nation (Rev. 2:13).

Lord, remove every synagogue of Satan from
my city, region, and nation (Rev. 3:9).

I bind and rebuke all wrath of the devil
directed against my life (Rev. 12:12).

Devil, I resist you. Flee (James 4:7).

I am sober and vigilant against my
adversary, the devil (1 Pet. 5:8).

REBUKING THE ENEMY

Satan, the Lord rebukes thee (Zech. 3:2).

Let the enemy perish at Your rebuke, O Lord (Ps. 80:16).

Let the enemy flee at Your rebuke, O Lord (Ps. 104:7).

I rebuke all the winds and storms of the enemy
sent against my life (Mark 4:39).

Rebuke the company of the spearmen and the multitude
of the bulls until they submit (Ps. 68:30).

Rebuke those that rush at me, and let them flee away (Isa. 17:13).

Rebuke the devourer for my sake (Mal. 3:11).

Rebuke the horse and chariot, and let them
fall into a deep sleep (Ps. 76:6).

I rebuke every unclean spirit that would attempt
to operate in my life (Luke 9:42).

I rebuke the proud spirits that are cursed (Ps. 119:21).

I release furious rebukes upon the enemy (Ezek. 25:17).

Let the blast of your nostrils rebuke the enemy (2 Sam. 22:16).

Rebuke the enemy with flames of fire (Isa. 66:15).

Let a thousand flee at my rebuke, O Lord (Isa. 30:17).

Rebuke every sea that would try to close upon my life (Ps. 106:9).

Devil, I rebuke you. Hold your peace, and come out (Mark 1:25).

SPEAKING TO MOUNTAINS

I speak to every mountain in my life and command it
to be removed and cast into the sea (Mark 11:23).

I speak to every financial mountain to be removed
from my life in the name of Jesus.

Let every evil mountain hear the voice of the
Lord and be removed (Mic. 6:2).

I prophesy to the mountains and command them to hear
the Word of the Lord and be removed (Ezek. 36:4).

Let the mountains tremble at the presence of God (Hab. 3:10).

I contend with every mountain and command
them to hear my voice (Mic. 6:1).

Lay the mountain of Esau (the flesh) to waste (Mal. 1:3).

Put forth Your hand, O Lord, and overturn
the mountains by the roots (Job 28:9).

I speak to every mountain of debt to be
removed and cast into the sea.

Lord, You are against every destroying mountain (Jer. 51:25).

Let the mountains melt at Your presence, O God (Judg. 5:5).

Make waste the evil mountains in my life, O Lord (Isa. 42:15).

I thresh every mountain, I beat them small, and
I make the hills as chaff (Isa. 41:15).

Every mountain in my way will become a plain (Zech. 4:7).

Releasing the Spoilers

Let the counsel of the wicked be spoiled (Job 12:17).

Lead the princes of darkness away spoiled (Job 12:19).

Let the stouthearted be spoiled (Ps. 76:5).

I bind the enemy, strip him of his armor,
and divide his spoils (Luke 11:22).

I release the spoilers to come upon Babylon
and destroy her (Jer. 51:53).

I release the spoilers to come upon the high
places in the name of Jesus (Jer. 12:12).

Lord, You have spoiled principalities and powers (Col. 2:15).

I spoil the enemy and take back his goods
in the name of Jesus (Exod. 12:36).

I spoil the tents of the enemy in the name of Jesus (1 Sam. 17:53).

I spoil those that have attempted to spoil me (Ezek. 39:10).

The enemy will not spoil me, but he will be spoiled (Isa. 33:1).

Let the palaces and headquarters of darkness be
spoiled in the name of Jesus (Amos 3:11).

Let the proud spirits be spoiled in the name of Jesus (Zech. 11:3).

I release the cankerworm to spoil the works of
darkness in the name of Jesus (Nah. 3:16).

Let the fortresses of darkness be spoiled in
the name of Jesus (Hos. 10:14).

SECTION 3

CONFRONTING the ENEMY'S TACTICS

WE ARE NOT TO BE IGNORANT OF THE DEVIL'S TACTICS. We can overcome all the schemes of the devil. The devil is a schemer. A *scheme* is a plan, design, or program of action. The Bible talks about the wiles of the devil (Eph. 6:11). A *wile* is a trick or a trap. A *trap* is a snare.

Warfare involves tactics and strategies. The greatest generals are great tacticians and strategists. You cannot win without a strategy. Don't allow the enemy to strategize against you. Overcome and destroy his strategies through prayer.

Traps and snares are hidden. People fall into traps unknowingly. We are delivered from the snare of the fowler. A *fowler* is a hunter. Satan is the hunter of souls. We can release ourselves and others through prayer.

The main tactic of the enemy is deception. He is a liar and the father of lies. The Word of God exposes the tactics of the enemy. God is light, and His Word is light. The light exposes the enemy and tears away the darkness.

Multitudes of people are deceived by the enemy. There are hosts of lying and deceiving spirits that work under the authority of Satan. These spirits include delusion, deception, lying, seducing, blinding, error, and guile. Our praying can strip the power of these deceiving spirits and cause the eyes of people to be opened.

David prayed against the enemy conspiracies of the wicked. The psalms are filled with references to the plans of his enemies to overthrow him. His prayers were the key in destroying these plans and bringing him deliverance. David prayed for his enemies to be scattered, confused, exposed, and destroyed.

David's struggles were with natural enemies. Behind these natural enemies were spiritual ones that were opposed to the Davidic kingdom. Jesus was to come from this line and sit upon this throne. David was fighting something beyond the natural. Through the Holy Spirit he was contending with the powers of darkness that were set against the arrival of the kingdom of God.

These powers were also manifested through Herod, who attempted to kill the coming Messiah. Herod was driven by spirits of fear and murder. He was used by Satan to attempt to abort the coming kingdom. However, the Holy Spirit had already been loosed through the prayers of David, and David's throne was secure.

Many of these warfare prayers are taken from the psalms of David. Jesus is the Son of David. He sits on the throne of David. David's prophetic prayers were weapons against the enemy's attempt to stop the promised seed. David's victories in prayer opened the way for his throne to continue. The throne of wickedness was unable to overcome the throne of righteousness.

God taught David. He became the warrior king. His victories caused his kingdom to be established. His victory over the house of Saul came after a long war (2 Sam. 3:1). Don't become discouraged in prayer. Continue to pray. You will become stronger, and the enemy will become weaker.

David consumed his enemies (Ps. 18:37–40). He did not turn until they were destroyed. We must see our spiritual enemies completely destroyed. We must pursue the enemy. *To pursue* means "to follow in order to overtake or capture." It means "to chase with hostile intent." We cannot be passive when it comes to warfare.

David's victories prepared the way for Solomon. Solomon enjoyed peace and prosperity. Solomon's name means "peace." *Peace* is the Hebrew word *shalom*. *Shalom* means "peace, prosperity, favor, health, and well-being." Your victories over the enemy will release *shalom*. You will experience greater levels of peace and prosperity.

QUENCHING THE FIRE OF THE ENEMY

I quench with the shield of faith every fiery dart
the enemy sends my way (Eph. 6:16).

I quench every fiery dart of jealousy, envy, anger, bitterness,
and rage sent against my life in the name of Jesus.

I quench every firebrand sent against my life by
the enemy in the name of Jesus (Isa. 7:4).

I bind and rebuke all spirits of jealousy directed
against my life in the name of Jesus.

I quench every fire the enemy would throw into my
sanctuary in the name of Jesus (Ps. 74:7).

I bind and cast out every fiery serpent sent against
my life in the name of Jesus (Isa. 30:6).

I quench every burning lamp that comes from
the leviathan's mouth (Job 41:19).

I will not be burned by the fire of the enemy (Isa. 43:2).

I overcome every fiery trial sent against
my life by the enemy (1 Pet. 1:7).

The enemy will not be able to burn up my harvest (2 Sam. 14:30).

I quench every fire of wickedness sent against
my life in the name of Jesus (Isa. 9:18).

I quench all ungodly words spoken against my
life in the name of Jesus (Prov. 16:27).

I quench every torch the enemy would use against
my life in the name of Jesus (Zech. 12:6).

I quench all gossip directed against my life
in the name of Jesus (Prov. 26:20).

The enemy's flame will not kindle upon me (Isa. 43:2).

BREAKING CURSES AND RELEASING THE BLESSINGS OF GOD

I am redeemed from the curse through
the blood of Jesus (Gal. 3:13).

I am the seed of Abraham, and his blessing is mine (Gal. 3:14).

I choose blessing instead of cursing and life
instead of death (Deut. 11:26).

I break and release myself from all generational
curses and iniquities as a result of the sins of
my ancestors in the name of Jesus.

I break and release myself from all curses on both
sides of my family back sixty generations.

I break all curses of witchcraft, sorcery, and
divination in the name of Jesus.

I break and release myself from all curses of
pride and rebellion in the name of Jesus.

I break and release myself from all curses of death
and destruction in the name of Jesus.

I break and rebuke all curses of sickness
and infirmity in the name of Jesus.

I break and release myself from all curses of
poverty, lack, and debt in the name of Jesus.

I break and release myself from all curses
of rejection in the name of Jesus.

I break and release myself from all curses of doublemindedness
and schizophrenia in the name of Jesus.

I break and release myself from all curses of
Jezebel and Ahab in the name of Jesus.

I break and release myself from all curses of
divorce and separation in the name of Jesus.

I break and release myself from all curses of lust
and perversion in the name of Jesus.

I break and release myself from all curses of confusion
and mental illness in the name of Jesus.

I break and release myself from all curses
of idolatry in the name of Jesus.

I break and release myself from all curses causing
accidents and premature death in the name of Jesus.

I break and release myself from all curses of
wandering and vagabond in the name of Jesus.

I break and release myself from all spoken curses
and negative words spoken against me by others
and by those in authority, and I bless them.

I break and release myself from all self-inflicted curses by
negative words I have spoken in the name of Jesus.

I command every demon hiding and operating behind
a curse to come out in the name of Jesus.

PRAYERS TO OVERCOME SATANIC AND DEMONIC CONSPIRACIES

I loose confusion against every satanic and
demonic conspiracy against my life.

Let the secret counsel of the wicked be turned into foolishness.

Let those gathered against me be scattered.

Send out Your lightning, O Lord, and scatter the enemy.

Destroy, O Lord, and divide their tongues (Ps. 55:9).

No weapon formed against me shall prosper. The gates
and plans of hell shall not prevail against me.

I overcome every strategy of hell against my life.

Every strategy of hell is exposed and brought to light.

I receive the plans of God for my life, thoughts of peace
and not evil to bring me to an expected end.

I am delivered from every satanic trap and plot against my life.

I release the whirlwind to scatter those
who would conspire against me.

Let those who devise my hurt be turned
back and brought to confusion.

Let the nets they have hid catch themselves, and
into that very destruction let them fall.

I bind and rebuke every spirit of Sanballat and
Tobiah in the name of Jesus (Neh. 6:1–6).

Hide me from the secret counsel of the wicked (Ps. 64:2).

OVERCOMING AND DIVIDING DEMONIC CONFEDERACIES

I break and divide every demonic confederacy
against my life in the name of Jesus.

I loose confusion into every demonic confederacy directed
against my life, family, and church in the name of Jesus.

Divide and scatter them that are joined together against me.

I bind and rebuke all demonic reinforcements
sent by Satan to attack my life.

Make the ruling spirits of these confederacies be like
Oreb, Zeeb, Zebah, and Zalmunna (Ps. 83:5–11).

O my God, make them like the wheel, as the
stubble before the wind (Ps. 83:13).

Persecute them with Thy tempest, and make
them afraid with Thy storm (Ps. 83:15).

Let them be confounded and troubled forever. Let them be put to shame and perish (Ps. 83:17).

Loose confusion, and let them attack each other in the name of Jesus (2 Chron. 20:23).

PRAYERS OVER HIGH PLACES

Lord, You created the high places for Your glory. Let not the enemy control the high places.

I bind the prince of the power of the air (Eph. 2:2).

I bind the powers of darkness that would control the airwaves and release filth, violence, and witchcraft through the media in the name of Jesus.

I take authority over the princes of media in the name of Jesus (Dan. 8:20).

I bind spiritual wickedness in high places (Eph. 6:12).

Lord, destroy the idols in high places (Lev. 26:30).

I pluck down the high places of the enemy (Num. 33:52).

I am a king, and I break down the high places in the name of Jesus (2 Kings 18:4).

I remove Nehushtan (previous moves of God that have become idols) from the high places (2 Kings 18:4).

I remove the religious spirits from the high places (2 Kings 23:8).

Let the high place of Tophet be removed (Jer. 7:31).

Let Your holy fire burn up the high places.

Let the high places of witchcraft be destroyed in the name of Jesus (2 Chron. 28:4).

Destroy all false worship in the high places (2 Chron. 28:25).

Let the high places be purged through Your anointing (2 Chron. 34:3).

Remove every false ministry in high places (1 Kings 12:31).

Remove all strange gods from the high places (2 Chron. 14:3).

Remove every satanic altar erected in the
high places (2 Chron. 14:3).

Let all high places established by any ungodly ruler
be removed in the name of Jesus (2 Kings 23:19).

Let all the high places of Baal be broken down (Jer. 19:5).

I prophesy to the ancient high places and
dispossess the enemy (Ezek. 36:1–3).

Let righteous men with Your wisdom sit in the high
governmental places of my city and nation (Prov. 9:3).

I will walk upon the high places (Hab. 3:19).

Let every high place of wickedness that has not
been removed be removed (1 Kings 15:14).

Let me ride upon the high places of the earth, and let me
eat the increase of the fields, and let me suck honey out of
the rock and oil out of the flinty rock (Deut. 32:13).

Let all high places built by my ancestors be removed (2 Kings 18:4).

Let not the high places our spiritual fathers
destroyed be rebuilt (2 Chron. 33:3).

Let the high places be desolate (Ezek. 6:6).

I tread upon the high places of the wicked (Deut. 33:29).

I break the power of any sacrifice done in
the high places (1 Kings 3:2).

I walk in the spirit of Josiah to deal with
the high places (2 Chron. 34:3).

Lord, open rivers in high places (Isa. 41:18).

PRAYERS OVER GATES

Through Jesus let me possess the gate of the enemy (Gen. 22:17).

Establish the gates of praise in my life (Isa. 60:18).

I release battering rams against the gates of hell (Ezek. 21:22).

The gates of hell cannot prevail against me (Matt. 16:18).

Let the gates of my life and city be open
to the King of glory (Ps. 24:7).

Open to me the gates of righteousness
that I may enter in (Ps. 118:19).

Strengthen the bars of my gates (Ps. 147:13).

Break the gates of brass, and cut in sunder
the bars of iron (Isa. 45:2).

Open before me the gates, that I may go in and receive the treasure
of darkness and hidden riches of secret places (Isa. 45:1–3).

I rebuke every enemy in the gates (Ps. 127:5).

Let all the gates of my life and city be
repaired through the Holy Spirit.

Let the valley gate be repaired (Neh. 2:13).

Let the gate of the fountain (represents the flow
of the Holy Spirit) be repaired (Neh. 2:14).

Let the sheep gate (represents the apostolic) be repaired (Neh. 3:1).

Let the fish gate (represents evangelism) be repaired (Neh. 3:3).

Let the old gate (represents moves of the
past) be repaired (Neh. 3:6).

Let the dung gate (represents deliverance) be repaired (Neh. 3:14).

Let the water gate (represents preaching and
teaching) be repaired (Neh. 3:26).

Let the east gate (represents the glory) be
repaired (Neh. 3:29; Ezek. 43:1–2).

Let the waters flow through the utter gate into my life, past
my ankles, past my loins, and past my neck (Ezek. 47:1–5).

Make my gates of carbuncles (Isa. 54:12).

My gates will be open continually to receive blessings (Isa. 60:11).

I command the north gate, the south gate, the east gate, and
the west gate to open in my city to the King of glory.

I rebuke all enemies that would stand at the gates
and try to stop salvation from entering in.

I pray for the apostolic gatekeepers of my city
to arise and take their place (Lam. 5:14).

Let the gates of my life and city be shut to uncleanness, witchcraft,
drugs, perversion, and wickedness in the name of Jesus.

I pray for the gateway cities in my nation to become
gateways of righteousness and not iniquity.

Lord, raise up bethel churches that will be
the gate of heaven (Gen. 28:17).

Lord, raise up apostolic gate churches that will
usher presence and revelation into my region.

PRAYERS AGAINST IDOLS

Let any idol in my life or nation be destroyed and
burned with Your fire (1 Kings 15:13).

Lord, cut down all the idols in the land (2 Chron. 34:7).

Let the familiar spirits, wizards, and idols be
taken out of the land (2 Kings 23:24).

Let the idols be confounded and the images
be broken in pieces (Jer. 50:2).

Let men throw away their idols and turn to You, O Lord (Isa. 31:7).

I renounce all idolatry in my bloodline and break all curses of idolatry in the name of Jesus (2 Kings 21:21).

Lord, put the names of the idols out of the land (Zech. 13:2).

I will keep myself from idols (1 John 5:21).

Abolish the idols in America and the nations (Isa. 2:18).

Lord, expose all idols as lying vanities (Zech. 10:2).

I renounce all covetousness; I will not serve the god of mammon (Col. 3:5).

Let Babylon, the mother of harlots and abominations of the earth, fall in the name of Jesus (Rev. 17:5).

Lord, cleanse the pollution of idols from the land (Acts 15:20).

Sprinkle clean water upon me, and cleanse me from all filthiness, and cleanse me from all idols (Ezek. 36:25).

Let me not go astray after any idol (Ezek. 44:10).

Let all false gods and idols (including humans) be removed from my life in the name of Jesus.

I will put no other gods before You, Lord (Exod. 20:3).

PRAYERS THAT DESTROY OPPRESSION

I rebuke and cast out any spirit that would attempt to oppress me in the name of Jesus.

Jesus, You went about doing good and healing all those oppressed of the devil (Acts 10:38).

I strip all power from spirits that would oppress me (Eccles. 4:1).

I rebuke and cast out all spirits of poverty that would oppress me (Eccles. 5:8).

I rebuke all spirits of madness and confusion that would attempt to oppress my mind in the name of Jesus (Eccles. 7:7).

O Lord, undertake for me against all my oppressors (Isa. 38:14).

Lord, You are my refuge from the oppressor (Ps. 9:9).

Deliver me from the wicked that would oppress me and from my deadly enemies that would surround me (Ps. 17:9).

Deliver me from oppressors that seek after my soul (Ps. 54:3).

Break in pieces the oppressor (Ps. 72:4).

I rebuke and cast out all spirits of affliction, sorrow, and anything attempting to bring me low in the name of Jesus (Ps. 107:39).

Leave me not to my oppressors (Ps. 119:121).

Let not the proud oppress me (Ps. 119:122).

Deliver me from the oppression of men (Ps. 119:134).

I rule over my oppressors (Ps. 14:2).

Let the oppressors be consumed out of the land (Isa. 16:4).

I rebuke the voice of the oppressor in the name of Jesus (Ps. 55:3).

I am established in righteousness, and I am far from oppression (Isa. 54:14).

Punish those who attempt to oppress me (Jer. 30:20).

The enemy will not take my inheritance through oppression (Ezek. 46:18).

Execute judgment against my oppressors (Ps. 146:7).

BREAKING THE POWER OF SCHIZOPHRENIA AND DOUBLEMINDEDNESS

(Based on the schizophrenia revelation of Ida Mae Hammond.)

I bind and rebuke every spirit that would attempt to distort, disturb, or disintegrate the development of my personality in the name of Jesus.

I break all curses of schizophrenia and doublemindedness on my family in the name of Jesus.

I bind and rebuke the spirit of doublemindedness in the name of Jesus (James 1:8).

I bind and take authority over the strongmen of rejection and rebellion and separate them in the name of Jesus.

I bind and cast out the spirits of rejection, fear of rejection, and self-rejection in the name of Jesus.

I bind and cast out all spirits of lust, fantasy lust, harlotry, and perverseness in the name of Jesus.

I bind and cast out all spirits of insecurity and inferiority in the name of Jesus.

I bind and cast out all spirits of self-accusation and compulsive confession in the name of Jesus.

I bind and cast out all spirits of fear of judgment, self-pity, false compassion, and false responsibility in the name of Jesus.

I bind and cast out all spirits of depression, despondency, despair, discouragement, and hopelessness in the name of Jesus.

I bind and cast out all spirits of guilt, condemnation, unworthiness, and shame in the name of Jesus.

I bind and cast out all spirits of perfection, pride, vanity, ego, intolerance, frustration, and impatience in the name of Jesus.

I bind and cast out all spirits of unfairness, withdrawal, pouting, unreality, fantasy, daydreaming, and vivid imagination in the name of Jesus.

I bind and cast out all spirits of self-awareness, timidity, loneliness, and sensitivity in the name of Jesus.

I bind and cast out all spirits of talkativeness, nervousness, tension, and fear in the name of Jesus.

I bind and cast out all spirits of self-will, selfishness, and stubbornness in the name of Jesus.

I bind and cast out the spirit of accusation in the name of Jesus.

I bind and cast out all spirits of self-delusion, self-deception, and self-seduction in the name of Jesus.

I bind and cast out all spirits of judgment, pride, and unteachableness in the name of Jesus.

I bind and cast out all spirits of control and possessiveness in the name of Jesus.

I bind and cast out the root of bitterness in the name of Jesus.

I bind and cast out all spirits of hatred, resentment, violence, murder, unforgiveness, anger, and retaliation in the name of Jesus.

I bind and cast out spirits of paranoia, suspicion, distrust, persecution, confrontation, and fear in the name of Jesus.

PRAYERS AND DECREES THAT BREAK THE POWERS OF DARKNESS

Let the Assyrian be broken in my land (Isa. 14:25).

Break in pieces the gates of brass, and cut the bars of iron (Isa. 45:2).

I break every yoke from off my neck, and I burst all the bonds in the name of Jesus (Jer. 30:8).

Break them with the rod of iron, and dash them in pieces like a potter's vessel (Ps. 2:9).

Break the arm of the wicked (Ps. 10:15).

Break their teeth, O God, in their mouths. Break the teeth of the young lions (Ps. 58:6).

Let the oppressor be broken in pieces (Ps. 72:4).

Let the arms of the wicked be broken (Ps. 37:17).

Let the horns of the wicked be broken (Dan. 8:8).

Let the kingdoms of darkness be broken (Dan. 11:4).

Let the foundations of the wicked be broken (Ezek. 30:4).

Let the kingdoms of Babylon be broken (Jer. 51:58).

Let all the bows of the wicked be broken (Ps. 37:14).

I break in pieces the horse and the rider (Jer. 51:21).

I break in pieces the chariot and the rider (Jer. 51:21).

I break in pieces the captains and the rulers (Jer. 51:23).

Let Your Word out of my mouth be like a hammer that breaks the rocks in pieces (Jer. 23:29).

Break down every wall erected by the enemy against my life (Ezek. 13:14).

I break down every altar erected by the enemy against my life in the name of Jesus (Hos. 10:2).

Let the idols and images of the land be broken by Your power, O Lord (Deut. 7:5).

I break and disannul every demonic covenant made by my ancestors in the name of Jesus (Isa. 28:18).

Prayers Against the Spirit of Destruction

I bind and cast out the spirit of Apollyon (Abaddon) in the name of Jesus (Rev. 9:11).

I am redeemed from destruction (Ps. 103:4).

I break all curses of destruction in my family and bloodline in the name of Jesus.

I renounce all pride that would open the door for destruction (Prov. 16:18).

Rescue my soul from destructions (Ps. 35:17).

Send Your Word, and deliver me from any destruction (Ps. 107:20).

The destroyer cannot come into my life or family in the name of Jesus (Exod. 12:23).

The destroyer cannot destroy my prosperity (Job 15:21).

I am delivered from destruction that wastes at noonday (Ps. 91:6).

There is no wasting or destruction within my borders (Isa. 60:18).

I will enter in at the straight gate, and I will not walk in the path that leads to destruction (Matt. 7:13).

I bind the spirit of mammon that leads to destruction (1 Tim. 6:9–10).

I will keep my mouth and avoid destruction (Prov. 18:7).

I bind and rebuke the spirit of poverty that leads to destruction (Prov. 10:15).

I rebuke all destruction from my gates in the name of Jesus (Isa. 24:12).

Closing Breaches and Hedges

I close up any breach in my life that would give Satan and demons access in the name of Jesus (Eccles. 10:8).

I pray for every broken hedge in my life to be
restored in the name of Jesus (Eccles. 10:8).

I stand in the gap and make up the hedge (Ezek. 22:30).

I repent and receive forgiveness for any sin that has opened the
door for any spirit to enter and operate in my life (Eph. 4:27).

I am a rebuilder of the wall and a repairer of the breach (Isa. 58:12).

I renounce all crooked speech that would cause a
breach in the name of Jesus (Prov. 15:4).

Bind up all my breaches, O Lord (Isa. 30:26).

Let every breach be stopped in the name of Jesus (Neh. 4:7).

Let my walls be salvation and my gates praise (Isa. 60:18).

I pray for a hedge of protection around my mind, body,
finances, possessions, and family in the name of Jesus.

DESTROYING EVIL CAULDRONS (POTS)

I rebuke and destroy every wicked cauldron
in the name of Jesus (Ezek. 11:11–12).

I rebuke and destroy every seething pot or cauldron stirred
up by the enemy against my life, city, or nation (Job 41:20).

Let every wicked cauldron in my city be
broken in the name of Jesus.

I break every witchcraft cauldron stirred up by
witches and warlocks in the name of Jesus.

Lord, visit every witch and warlock in my region, and
convict. Let them repent, turn to You, and be saved.

I am delivered from the boiling pot in the
name of Jesus (Ezek. 24:1–5).

Lord, bring me out of the midst of every cauldron (Ezek. 11:7).

The enemy will not eat my flesh, break my bones,
and put me in his cauldron (Mic. 3:3).

Lord, deliver and protect me from every pot of
evil in the name of Jesus (Jer. 1:13–14).

Lord, deliver me from the boiling pot of pride (Job 41:31).

DESTROYING YOKES AND REMOVING BURDENS

I remove all false burdens placed on me by people, leaders,
or churches in the name of Jesus (1 Thess. 2:6).

I remove all heavy burdens placed on my life
by the enemy in the name of Jesus.

Let your anointing break the enemy's burden from off
my neck, and let every yoke be destroyed (Isa. 10:27).

Remove my shoulder from every burden (Ps. 81:6).

I cast my cares upon the Lord (1 Pet. 5:7).

I cast my burdens upon the Lord, and He sustains me (Ps. 55:22).

Lord, break the yoke of the enemy's burden, and break the staff
and the rod of the oppressor as in the day of Midian (Isa. 9:4).

Let every yoke of poverty be destroyed in the name of Jesus.

Let every yoke of sickness be destroyed in the name of Jesus.

Let every yoke of bondage be destroyed
in the name of Jesus (Gal. 5:1).

Let every unequal yoke be broken in the name of Jesus (2 Cor. 6:14).

I destroy every yoke and burden of religion and legalism on
my life by religious leaders in the name of Jesus (Matt. 23:4).

Let every burdensome stone be released from
my life in the name of Jesus (Zech. 12:3).

I take upon my life the yoke and burden of Jesus (Matt. 11:30).

Section 4

DESTROYING the ENEMY'S FORCES

Jesus came to destroy the works of the devil (1 John 3:8). The works of the devil are carried out by his forces. Satan's kingdom consists of principalities, powers, rulers of the darkness of this world, and spiritual wickedness in high places. There are different kinds of demons and different levels of wickedness. We can destroy the wicked early (Ps. 101:8). We can destroy them that hate us (Ps. 18:40).

Satan is rendered helpless when his forces are destroyed. We have authority to bind the strongman and strip him of his armor. Israel was sent into Canaan to destroy different nations, which are pictures of kingdoms that possessed the land. Each kingdom represented a different type of stronghold God wanted His people to destroy.

Demons are also represented by different creatures. The diversity in the animal kingdom is a picture of the diversity in the kingdom of darkness. The Bible talks about serpents, scorpions, lions, jackals, bulls, foxes, owls, sea serpents, flies, and dogs. These represent different kinds of evil spirits that operate to destroy mankind. They are invisible to the natural eye. They are just as real, however, as natural creatures.

We must always remember that there are more with us than against us. The forces of light are far superior to the forces of darkness. Jesus is the Lord of the armies. The armies of heaven are fighting with the armies of earth. Releasing the angelic armies of heaven is an important strategy in warfare.

We can destroy and rout the forces of darkness in the heavens, the earth, the sea, and under the earth. These forces can operate through people, governments, economic systems, educational systems, and different structures set up by men. These forces can operate from different locations and in different territories.

The idols that men worship are made in the image of men, four-footed beasts, birds, and creeping things. Behind these idols are demons. These are evil spirits that manifest in the natural through idols. These gods (idols) are also male and female. The nations worship gods and goddesses. Jezebel is an example of a female principality.

The Bible uses strong words that pertain to warfare, including:

- *Abolish*—to end, cut, strike through (Isa. 2:18; 2 Tim. 1:10)

- *Beat down*—beat, bruise, violently strike, crush, destroy, discomfort, break down by violence, dismay, terrify (Judg. 9:45; 2 Kings 13:25; Ps. 18:42; Isa. 27:12; Jer. 46:5)

- *Break down*—deliver, break, rend in pieces, crush, destroy, to spoil (by breaking in pieces), pluck down, pull down, ruin, beat down, cast down, dash in pieces, disperse (Exod. 34:13; Lev. 26:19; Ps. 2:9; 10:15; 58:6; 72:4; Eccles. 3:3; Isa. 45:2; Jer. 28:4; Dan. 2:40)

- *Cast down*—to tear down, break down, destroy, overthrow, pull down, throw down, cast down to hell (Judg. 6:28, 30; Ps. 17:13; 89:44; 102:10; 147:6; Isa. 28:2; Jer. 8:12; Dan. 7:9; 8:10; 2 Cor. 4:9; 10:5; 2 Pet. 2:4)

- *Cast out*—to occupy by driving out the previous tenants and possessing their place, to seize, to rob, to inherit, to expel, to impoverish, to send away, to push away or down, cast away, to banish, to eject, send out, throw out (Exod. 34:24; Lev. 18:24; Deut. 6:19; 1 Kings 14:24; 2 Kings 16:3; Job 20:15; Ps. 5:10; Matt. 12:28; Mark 6:13; Luke 9:40; John 12:31; Rev. 12:9)

- *Chase (pursue)*—run after with hostile intent, put to flight, persecute (Lev. 26:7–8; Deut. 32:30; Ps. 18:37; 35:3; Isa. 17:13)

- *Confound (confuse)*—to be ashamed, disappointed, brought to confusion, put to shame (Ps. 35:4, 26; 40:14; 70:2, 13, 24; 83:17; 97:7; 109:29; 129:5; Jer. 17:18; 50:2)

- *Consume*—to end, consume away, destroy, make clean riddance, to eat up, devour, burn up (Deut. 7:16, 22; Ps. 37:20; 71:13; 104:35; 2 Thess. 2:8; Heb. 12:29)

- *Contend*—to grate, to anger, meddle, strive, stir up, grapple with, to defend, chide, rebuke, initiate a controversy (Deut. 2:24; Isa. 41:12; 49:25; Jer. 12:5; Jude 9)

- *Destroy*—to end, to cease, destroy utterly, make clean, waste, make accursed, tear down, beat down, break down, to devour, eat up (Lev. 26:30, 44; 20:17; 31:3; Ps. 5:6, 10; 18:40; 21:10; 28:5; 52:5; 55:9; 74:8; 101:8; 144:6; Prov. 15:25; Isa. 23:11; Jer. 1:10; Matt. 21:41; Mark 1:24; 9:22; John 10:10; 1 John 3:8)

- *Fight*—to consume, to battle, make war, overcome, prevail, struggle, contend with the adversary (Exod. 14:14; 17:9; Deut. 1:30; Josh. 10:25; Judg. 1:1, 3, 9;

Ps. 35:1; 144:1; Dan. 10:20; 1 Tim. 6:12; 2 Tim. 4:7; Heb. 10:32)

- *Prevail*—to enclose, to hold back, shut up, stop, be strong, put on strength, to overpower, restrain, bind, conquer (2 Chron. 14:11; Ps. 9:19; Isa. 42:13; Matt. 16:18)

- *Smite*—strike, beat, cast forth, slaughter, give stripes, wound, slay, push, defeat, inflict, dash, gore, hurt, put to the worse (Num. 25:17; Deut. 13:15; Josh. 7:3; Judg. 20:31; 1 Sam. 15:3; Isa. 19:22; Jer. 43:11; Acts 7:24; Rev. 11:6)

- *Wrestle*—to struggle, grapple (Gen. 30:8; 32:24; Eph. 6:12)

The Bible contains many words that speak of warfare. The Bible is filled with warfare. The history of man has been determined by wars. John saw war in heaven between Michael and his angels and Satan and his angels (Rev. 12:7). War requires warriors. Warriors must have the tenacity to overcome their enemies. Remember, God trains our hands to war and our fingers to fight (Ps. 144:1).

PRAYERS AGAINST DEMONIC PRINCES

Jesus, You have cast out the prince of this world and defeated him (John 12:31).

Jesus, You spoiled principalities and made an open show of them (Col. 2:15).

I bind the prince of the power of the air in the name of Jesus (Eph. 2:2).

I bind and rebuke Beelzebub, the prince of demons (Matt. 12:24).

I bind the principalities and powers in my region in the name of Jesus (Eph. 6:12).

I command the principalities to come down in the name of Jesus (Jer. 13:18).

Lord, release Your warrior angels against the demonic princes (Dan. 10:20).

Smite the princes as the days of old (Josh. 13:21).

Bring the iniquity of every profane prince to an end, and remove the diadem from his head (Ezek. 21:25–26).

Lead the princes away spoiled, and overthrow the mighty (Job 12:19).

Make the nobles like Oreb and like Zeeb, and all their princes like Zebah and Zalmunna (Ps. 83:11).

Pour contempt upon the demon princes (Ps. 107:40).

Cut off the spirits of princes (Ps. 76:12).

I rebuke and bind all princes that would speak against me (Ps. 119:23).

I rebuke and bind all princes that would persecute me (Ps. 119:161).

Bring the princes to nothing (Isa. 34:12).

Punish the princes with Your power (Zeph. 1:8).

PRAYERS AGAINST LEVIATHAN AND MARINE SPIRITS

O Lord, break the heads of the dragons in the waters (Ps. 74:13).

Cut off the head of every hydra in the name of Jesus.

Break the heads of leviathan in pieces (Ps. 74:14).

Punish leviathan, the piercing serpent, even leviathan the crooked serpent, with Your sore, great, and strong sword (Isa. 27:1).

Slay the dragon that is in the sea (Ps. 27:1).

I break all curses of pride and leviathan from my life in the name of Jesus.

Rip the scales of leviathan (Job 41:15).

Break the strength of leviathan's neck (Ps. 18:40).

Break the stony heart of leviathan and crush it to pieces (Job 41:24).

Break the teeth of leviathan and pluck the spoil out of his mouth (Job 41:15).

I put a hook in leviathan's nose, a cord around his tongue, and I bore a thorn in his jaw (Job 41:1–2).

Lord, You rule the sea and the waters by Your strength.

Do not let any evil waters overflow my life.

The channels of waters are seen at Your rebuke (Ps. 18:15).

Rebuke all proud and arrogant demons that are cursed (Ps. 119:21).

I bind every sea monster that would attack my life or region in the name of Jesus (Lam. 4:3).

Bring down the haughty demons by Your power.

Bring down the proud demons that have exalted themselves against Your people.

Scatter the proud in the imagination of their hearts.

God, You resist the proud. Your power is against
the high ones who have rebelled against You.

Let not the foot of pride come against me (Ps. 36:11).

Break the crown of pride (Isa. 28:1).

Break Rahab in pieces, as one that is slain. Scatter
Your enemies with Your strong arm (Ps. 89:10).

Let not leviathan oppress me (Ps. 119:122).

O Lord, render a reward to leviathan (Ps. 94:2).

Raise up a watch over leviathan (Job 7:12).

Let not the proud waters go over my soul (Ps. 124:5).

I rebuke and destroy every trap the devil
has set for me (Ps. 140:5).

Let the proud spirits stumble and fall (Jer. 50:32).

Break the pride of leviathan's power (Lev. 26:19).

Awake, awake. Put on strength, O arm of the Lord. I command
the helpers of Rahab to bow before the Lord (Isa. 51:9).

Let not the foot of pride come against me (Ps. 36:11).

I strip the scales of leviathan and take away
his armor (Job 41:15; Luke 11:22).

Cast abroad the rage of thy wrath and abase leviathan (Job 40:11).

Smite through leviathan with your understanding (Job 26:12).

Look on leviathan, and bring him low. Tread
him down in his place (Job 40:12).

Rebuke the bulls of Bashan (Ps. 22:12).

Let the mighty be spoiled; let the oaks
of Bashan howl (Zech. 11:2).

Bring Your people from Bashan; bring Your people
from the depths of the sea (Ps. 68:22).

Smite Bashan and the kingdom of Og (Ps. 135:10–11).

I bind and cast out all mind-control spirits of the octopus and squid in the name of Jesus.

Let the waters of the deep be dried up, and destroy every spirit of leviathan (Job 41:31; Isa. 44:27).

In the name of Jesus, I dry up your rivers, your seas, and your springs (Isa. 19:5).

I call for a drought upon leviathan's waters (Jer. 50:38; Jer. 51:36).

Prayers Against Jezebel

I loose the hounds of heaven against Jezebel (1 Kings 21:23).

I rebuke and bind the spirits of witchcraft, lust, seduction, intimidation, idolatry, and whoredom connected to Jezebel.

I release the spirit of Jehu against Jezebel and her cohorts (2 Kings 9:30–33).

I command Jezebel to be thrown down and eaten by the hounds of heaven.

I rebuke all spirits of false teaching, false prophecy, idolatry, and perversion connected with Jezebel (Rev. 2:20).

I loose tribulation against the kingdom of Jezebel (Rev. 2:22).

I cut off the assignment of Jezebel against the ministers of God (1 Kings 19:2).

I cut off and break the powers of every word released by Jezebel against my life.

I cut off Jezebel's table and reject all food from it (1 Kings 18:19).

I cut off and loose myself from all curses of Jezebel and spirits of Jezebel operating in my bloodline.

I cut off the assignment of Jezebel and her daughters to corrupt the church.

I rebuke and cut off the spirit of Athaliah that attempts to destroy the royal seed (2 Kings 11:1).

I come against the spirit of Herodias and cut off the assignment to kill the prophets (Mark 6:22–24).

I rebuke and cut off the spirit of whoredoms (Hos. 4:12).

I rebuke and cut off Jezebel and her witchcrafts in the name of Jesus (2 Kings 9:22).

I rebuke and cut off the harlot and mistress of witchcrafts and break her power over my life and family (Nah. 3:4).

I cut off witchcrafts out of the hands (Mic. 5:12).

I overcome Jezebel and receive power over the nations (Rev. 2:26).

Dealing With Spirits of the Desert

I speak to every desert in my life or ministry in the name of Jesus.

I bind and cast out any desert spirit sent against my life.

I bind and cast out every spirit of the desert owl, the desert fox, the desert dragon, the desert hyena, and the desert vulture in the name of Jesus (Isa. 34:11–15).

I bind and cast out every scorpion spirit of fear and torment in the name of Jesus (Deut. 8:15).

I bind and rebuke the screech owl in the name of Jesus (Isa. 34:14).

I bind and cast out every jackal in the name of Jesus (Ezek. 13:15).

I will not dwell in the wilderness but in a fruitful land (Isa. 35:1).

My desert shall blossom as a rose and bring forth abundant fruit (Isa. 35:1).

Release water in my dry places and streams in the desert (Isa. 35:6).

Let rivers flow into my desert places (Isa. 43:20).

I rebuke the beasts of the desert, every doleful creature, every satyr, and every dragon from operating in my life (Isa. 13:21–22).

Let your voice shake every wilderness place in my life (Ps. 29:8).

Let fatness drop upon my wilderness places (Ps. 65:11–12).

Let the spirits of the wilderness bow and lick the dust (Ps. 72:9).

I rebuke every pelican and owl of the wilderness (Ps. 102:6).

Turn the wilderness into a pool of water and the dry ground into water springs (Ps. 107:35).

Open rivers in high places, and fountains in the midst of the valleys, and make my wilderness places a pool of water and my dry places springs of water (Isa. 41:18).

Plant in my wilderness places the cedar, the shittah tree, the myrtle tree, the oil tree, the fir tree, the pine tree, and the box tree together (Isa. 41:19).

I renounce all rebellion that would open my life to desert spirits (Ps. 68:6).

I break every curse of trusting in man that would open my life to desert spirits (Jer. 17:5–6).

I prophesy to every dry bone in my life and command it to live (Ezek. 37:1–4).

My land shall not be termed desolate, but I am called Hephzi-bah, and my land Beulah (Isa. 62:4).

Make all my wilderness places like Eden, and my desert places like the garden of the Lord (Ps. 51:3).

Let every desolation in my life or bloodline be raised up in the name of Jesus (Isa. 61:4).

Revive me, and repair every desolation in my life (Ezra 9:9).

PRAYERS AGAINST DEMONIC HORSEMEN

Let the horse and rider be thrown into the sea (Exod. 15:1).

Break in pieces the horse and his rider. Break in pieces the chariot and his rider (Jer. 51:21).

I release the sword of the Lord upon the horses and chariots (Jer. 50:37).

I cut off the horses and destroy the chariots in the name of Jesus (Mic. 5:10).

Overthrow the chariots and those that ride them. Bring down the horses and their riders (Hag. 2:22).

Confound the riders on horses (Zech. 10:5).

Let the horses' heels be bitten, and let the riders fall backward (Gen. 49:17).

Let the chariot, the horse, the army, and the power lie down together and not be able to rise (Isa. 43:17).

Let the chariot and the horse be cast into a deep sleep at Your rebuke, O Lord (Ps. 76:6).

Make the horses afraid as the grasshopper (Job 39:19–20).

Let the chariots and horsemen be burned with Your fire (Nah. 2:13).

Smite the horses with astonishment and the riders with madness and blindness, O Lord (Zech. 12:4).

I bind and rebuke every black horse that would come against me in the name of Jesus (Rev. 6:5).

I bind and rebuke every red horse that would come against me in the name of Jesus (Rev. 6:4).

I bind and rebuke every pale horse that would come against me in the name of Jesus (Rev. 6:8).

Take away the strength of the demonic horsemen in the name of Jesus (Job 39:19).

Let the horses be cut by Your power, O Lord (2 Sam. 8:4).

I am Your goodly horse in the day of battle (Zech. 10:3).

PRAYERS AGAINST SPIRITS OF THE VALLEY

I bind and cast out all spirits that would attempt to keep me in a low place in the name of Jesus.

I break the chariots of the enemies of the valley in the name of Jesus (Judg. 1:19).

I rebuke and cast out the ravens of the valley in the name of Jesus (Prov. 30:17).

Lord, You are the God of the valleys. Cast out every valley spirit in the name of Jesus (1 Kings 20:28).

Let me be exalted and the spirits of the valley be smitten by Your power (2 Sam. 8:13).

I bind and rebuke every Goliath that would challenge me in the valley (1 Sam. 17:1–4).

Let all the giants of the valley be destroyed (Josh. 15:8).

Fight against the spirits of the valley, and let my enemies be avenged in the valley (Josh. 10:12–14).

Let every Achan in my life be destroyed in the valley (Josh. 7:24–26).

I loose myself from every Delilah spirit operating in the valley (Judg. 16:4).

Let all my valley places be blessed in the name of Jesus (2 Chron. 20:26).

Open a door of hope in all my valleys (Hos. 2:15).

I destroy every Edomite spirit in the valley in the name of Jesus (2 Kings 14:7).

Let water flow into every valley place of my life (Joel 3:18).

Let every valley place in my life be exalted (Luke 3:5).

I smite Amalek and destroy him in the valley (1 Sam. 15:3–5).

I smite all the Midianites in the valley (Judg. 6:33–34).

DEALING WITH SPIRIT BIRDS

I bind and rebuke any unclean and hateful bird sent against my life by the enemy in the name of Jesus (Rev. 18:2).

I exercise my dominion over the unclean fowl of the air in the name of Jesus (Ps. 8:8).

Let every spirit bird sent against me be taken in the snare (Eccles. 9:12).

I bind and rebuke every spiritual vulture in the name of Jesus (Isa. 34:15).

I bind the operation of the screech owl (night monster) from operating against me in the name of Jesus (Isa. 34:14).

I bind and rebuke the cormorant (the vomiting pelican) from operating against my life in the name of Jesus (Isa. 34:11).

I bind and rebuke the bittern from operating against my life in the name of Jesus (Isa. 34:11).

I bind and rebuke any raven sent against my life in the name of Jesus (Isa. 34:11).

I bind and rebuke any demonic eagle and hawk sent against my life, and I command their nests to be destroyed in the name of Jesus (Job 39:26–30).

I pray these unclean birds would be caged in the name of Jesus (Jer. 5:27).

I bind and rebuke any unclean bird that would attempt to nest in my life in the name of Jesus.

Let every wandering bird be cast out of its nest in the name of Jesus (Isa. 16:2).

Let Your presence drive every unclean bird
away from my life (Jer. 4:25–26).

Let every fowl of heaven operating against my life
be consumed in the name of Jesus (Zeph. 1:3).

Let these birds flee and fly away at Your rebuke (Jer. 9:10).

Let me walk in the path of wisdom that
no fowl knows (Job 28:7, 21).

I will not be afraid of the terror by night, and I rebuke every
night bird that would attempt to visit me at night (Ps. 91:5).

I am not a companion to owls (Job 30:29).

DELIVERANCE FROM LIONS

I rebuke every lion that would stoop and crouch down
to attack me in the name of Jesus (Gen. 49:9).

Through the strength of God, I break the jaws of the lion
and pluck the spoil out of his mouth (Judg. 14:5).

Deliver me from the paw of the lion (1 Sam. 17:37).

I rebuke the fierce lion that would hunt me (Job 10:16).

Don't let the lion tear my soul (Ps. 7:2).

I rebuke and expose any lion that would
wait secretly to catch me (Ps. 10:9).

I rebuke any lurking lions in the name of Jesus (Ps. 17:12).

I tread upon the lion in the name of Jesus (Ps. 91:3).

I walk in holiness, and no lion can dwell in my life (Isa. 35:9).

Deliver me from men who are like lions (1 Chron. 11:22).

Let the lion's whelps be scattered (Job 4:11).

Save me from the lion's mouth (Ps. 22:21).

Break the teeth of the lions (Ps. 58:6).

Deliver my soul from lions (Ps. 57:4).

Deliver me from the power of the lions (Dan. 6:7).

Deliver me out of the mouth of the lion (2 Tim. 4:17).

Let the Lion of the tribe of Judah roar
through me against my enemies.

Deliver me from the power of the lion.

DELIVERANCE FROM SERPENTS

Lord, bruise the head of every serpent that would
attack my life in the name of Jesus.

Punish the piercing serpent in the name of Jesus.

I bind and rebuke any serpent that would
try to deceive me (2 Cor. 11:3).

I release the rod of God to swallow up every serpent that
would come against me in the name of Jesus (Exod. 7:12).

Protect me from fiery serpents (Deut. 8:15).

I bind and rebuke every serpent that would try to
twist or coil around my life in the name of Jesus.

I bind and rebuke every python that would try to
squeeze out my prayer life in the name of Jesus.

I bind and rebuke every cobra that would
come against me in the name of Jesus.

I bind and rebuke every cockatrice that would come
against me in the name of Jesus (Isa. 14:29).

I bind and rebuke every flying serpent that would
attack my life in the name of Jesus (Isa. 27:1).

I bind and rebuke every sea serpent that would
attack my life in the name of Jesus (Isa. 27:1).

I have authority to tread upon serpents (Luke 10:19).

I am a believer, and I pick up serpents (Mark 16:18).

Let the fire of God drive out every serpent from my life (Acts 28:3).

I cast out every viper that would operate
in my life in the name of Jesus.

Deliverance From Flies

I bind and rebuke Beelzebub, the lord of the
flies, in the name of Jesus (Matt. 12:24).

I bind and cast out all flies that would attempt to affect
my anointing in the name of Jesus (Eccles. 10:1).

I bind and rebuke any swarm of flies that would come
against me in the name of Jesus (Ps. 78:45).

No flies can live in my life in the name of Jesus (Exod. 8:21).

I renounce and loose myself from any spiritual garbage
that would attract flies in the name of Jesus.

I rebuke every fly and every bee that would come
upon my land in the name of Jesus (Isa. 7:18).

Deliverance From Animalistic Spirits

I am delivered from the wild beasts of the desert (Isa. 34:14).

I rebuke the jackals that would attack my life,
city, or nation in the name of Jesus.

I rebuke the night wolves that would attack my life,
city, or nation in the name of Jesus (Hab. 1:8).

I rebuke every goat spirit of Pan, Faun,
and Satyr in the name of Jesus.

I rebuke the wild cats—leopards, lions, jaguars, which
represent higher occult powers—that would attack
my life, city, or nation in the name of Jesus.

I rebuke the hyenas that would attack my life, city, or nation in the name of Jesus (Isa. 34:14).

I rebuke and bind every wild dog (represents false religion, witchcraft, and perversion) that would hound my life in the name of Jesus (Ps. 22:16).

I bind and rebuke the bulls (represents strong rebellion) in the name of Jesus (Ps. 22:12).

I command all foxes that would destroy my fruit to leave my life in the name of Jesus.

SECTION 5

EXPERIENCING DELIVERANCE
and RELEASE

ISRAEL EXPERIENCED MANY DELIVERANCES IN ITS HISTORY. The nation of Israel began with a mighty deliverance. David the king received many deliverances. He called upon the Lord for deliverance and was heard (Ps. 34:4). God answers the cries and prayers of His people. God's deliverance is always a sign of His love and mercy. The word *salvation* means "deliverance." The Bible is filled with stories of deliverance and salvation.

One of the greatest revelations is the revelation of self-deliverance. We can loose ourselves from any control in darkness (Isa. 52:2). We can exercise power and authority for our own lives. Jesus told us to cast out the beam from our own eye (Luke 6:42). The term *cast out* is the same word used in reference to casting out demons (*ekballo*).

Take spiritual responsibility for your life. Don't depend on everyone else for your spiritual well-being. Confess the Word over your life. Pray strong prayers that rout the enemy. Do not allow self-pity to hold you back. Stir yourself up to prayer. This is a key to an overcoming life.

Those who experienced deliverance either came or were brought to Jesus. Someone had to take the initiative. It all begins with a decision. You cannot allow passivity to rob you of deliverance. You must open your mouth. Your deliverance is as close as your mouth.

There are many people frustrated with life. People who struggle can become overwhelmed by doubt and failure. Some are battling stress and pressure, which often lead to emotional and physical problems. Jesus spent a considerable amount of time ministering to the oppressed. Multitudes came to hear Him in order to be healed and delivered from evil spirits.

Deliverance is the children's bread. Every child of God has a right to enjoy the benefits of deliverance. Deliverance brings freedom and joy. We have seen thousands of believers set free from demons through authoritative prayer. Deliverance is a miracle ministry. You will see multiplied miracles through warfare prayer.

The breakthroughs you will see are supernatural. Healings will multiply. Long-term bondages will be destroyed. Hidden roots will be exposed and eliminated. Inexplicable problems will be solved. Stubborn obstacles will be removed. Cycles of failure will be broken.

Frustration and despair will be eliminated through warfare prayer. Discouragement and disappointment will be overcome. The puzzling problems of life will be taken away. Lasting peace can finally be experienced. The abundant life can be enjoyed.

Failures that cause bitterness are reversed through warfare prayer. Prosperity and success will come. Advancement will be seen in different areas of your life. You will experience success in relationships, finances, ministry, and projects. Deliverance is designed to eliminate the spiritual obstacles that impede progress. Deliverance makes the rough places smooth and the crooked places straight.

You can see the enemy routed from your life. You can live free from the bondages and oppressions of demons. You can experience victory through prayer. Your words and prayers have tremendous power to destroy the works of darkness.

Those who experience deliverance and release will see notable changes. Sometimes the change is progressive and sometimes instantaneous. The change, however, will be dramatic. There will be an increase of joy, liberty, peace, and success. This will result in a better spiritual life with an increase of strength and holiness.

Patience is necessary to see breakthrough. God promised Israel that He would drive the enemy out little by little (Deut. 7:22; Exod. 23:29–30). Unless you understand this principle, you will become weary in praying for some people, and you will become discouraged in your own deliverance. The more freedom you will receive, the more you need to grow and possess your land.

You have the authority to bind and loose (Matt. 18:18). *Webster's* dictionary defines the word *bind* as "to make secure by tying; to confine, restrain, or restrict *as* if with bonds: to constrain with legal authority: to exert a restraining or compelling effect." It also means "to arrest, apprehend, handcuff, lead captive, take charge of, lock up, restrain, check, or put a stop to." Binding is done by legal authority. We have legal authority in the name of Jesus to bind the works of darkness.

The works of darkness encompass sin, iniquity, perversion, sickness, disease, infirmity, death, destruction, curses, witchcraft, sorcery, divination, poverty, lack, strife, lust, pride, rebellion, fear, torment, and confusion. We have legal authority to put a stop to these things in our lives and in the lives of those we minister to.

Loose means "to untie, to free from restraint, to detach, to disjoin, divorce, separate, unhitch, get free, get loose, escape, break away, unbind, unchain, unfetter, free, release, unlock, liberate, disconnect, or forgive."

People need to be loosed from curses, evil inheritance,

familiar spirits, sin, guilt, shame, condemnation, control, domination, manipulation, intimidation, mind control, religious control, sickness, disease, deception, false teaching, sin, habits, worldliness, carnality, demons, tradition, ungodly soul ties, ungodly pledges, ungodly vows, spoken words, hexes, vexes, jinxes, trauma, and cults. We have legal authority in the name of Jesus to loose ourselves and others to whom we minister from these destroying influences.

Prayers for Self-Deliverance

I break all generational curses of pride, rebellion, lust, poverty, witchcraft, idolatry, death, destruction, failure, sickness, infirmity, fear, schizophrenia, and rejection in the name of Jesus.

I command all generational and hereditary spirits operating in my life through curses to be bound and cast out in the name of Jesus.

I command all spirits of lust, perversion, adultery, fornication, uncleanness, and immorality to come out of my sexual character in the name of Jesus.

I command all spirits of hurt, rejection, fear, anger, wrath, sadness, depression, discouragement, grief, bitterness, and unforgiveness to come out of my emotions in the name of Jesus.

I command all spirits of confusion, forgetfulness, mind control, mental illness, doublemindedness, fantasy, pain, pride, and memory recall to come out of my mind in the name of Jesus.

I break all curses of schizophrenia and command all spirits of doublemindedness, rejection, rebellion, and root of bitterness to come out in the name of Jesus.

I command all spirits of guilt, shame, and condemnation to come out of my conscience in the name of Jesus.

I command all spirits of pride, stubbornness, disobedience, rebellion, self-will, selfishness, and arrogance to come out of my will in the name of Jesus.

I command all spirits of addiction to come out of my appetite in the name of Jesus.

I command all spirits of witchcraft, sorcery, divination, and occult to come out in the name of Jesus.

I command all spirits operating in my head, eyes, mouth, tongue, and throat to come out in the name of Jesus.

I command all spirits operating in my chest and lungs to come out in the name of Jesus.

I command all spirits operating in my back and spine to come out in the name of Jesus.

I command all spirits operating in my stomach, navel, and abdomen to come out in the name of Jesus.

I command all spirits operating in my heart, spleen, kidneys, liver, and pancreas to come out in the name of Jesus.

I command all spirits operating in my sexual organs to come out in the name of Jesus.

I command all spirits operating in my hands, arms, legs, and feet to come out in the name of Jesus.

I command all demons operating in my skeletal system, including my bones, joints, knees, and elbows, to come out in the name of Jesus.

I command all spirits operating in my glands and endocrine system to come out in the name of Jesus.

I command all spirits operating in my blood and circulatory systems to come out in the name of Jesus.

I command all spirits operating in my muscles and muscular system to come out in the name of Jesus.

I command all religious spirits of doubt, unbelief, error, heresy, and tradition that came in through religion to come out in the name of Jesus.

I command all spirits from my past that are hindering my present and future to come out in the name of Jesus.

I command all ancestral spirits that entered through my ancestors to come out in the name of Jesus.

I command all hidden spirits hiding in any part of my life to come out in the name of Jesus.

PRAYERS FOR PROSPERITY AND FINANCIAL RELEASE

I break all assignments of the enemy against my finances in the name of Jesus.

I break all curses of poverty, lack, debt, and failure in the name of Jesus.

I seek first the kingdom of God and His righteousness, and all things are added unto me (Matt. 6:33).

I rebuke and cast out all spirits of the cankerworm, palmerworm, caterpillar, and locust that would eat up my blessings in the name of Jesus (Joel 2:25).

Lord, teach me to profit, and lead me in the way I should go (Isa. 48:17).

You are Jehovah-Jireh, my provider (Gen. 22:14).

You are El Shaddai, the God of more than enough.

Wealth and riches are in my house because I fear You and delight greatly in Your commandments (Ps. 112:1–3).

The blessing of the Lord upon my life makes me rich.

I am blessed coming in and blessed going out.

I am God's servant, and He takes pleasure in my prosperity (Ps. 35:27).

Jesus, You became poor, that through Your poverty I might be rich (2 Cor. 8:9).

I meditate on the Word day and night, and whatever I do prospers (Ps. 1:3).

Let peace be within my walls and prosperity within my palace (Ps. 122:7).

I will prosper through the prophets and prophetic ministry (Ezra 6:14).

I believe the prophets, and I prosper (2 Chron. 20:20).

I am Your servant, Lord. Prosper me (Neh. 1:11).

The God of heaven will prosper me (Neh. 2:20).

I live in the prosperity of the King (Jer. 23:5).

Through Your favor I will be a prosperous person (Gen. 39:2).

Lord, You have called me, and You will make
my way prosperous (Isa. 48:15).

I pray in secret, and You reward me openly (Matt. 6:6).

I fast in secret, and You reward me openly (Matt. 6:18).

You reward me because I diligently seek You (Heb. 11:6).

Lord, release the wealth of the wicked into my hands (Prov. 13:22).

Lord, bring me into a wealthy place (Ps. 66:12).

I give, and it is given to me—good measure, pressed
down, shaken together, and running over (Luke 6:38).

Open the floodgates of heaven over my life, and I receive
more than I have enough room to receive (Mal. 3:10).

Let every hole in my bag be closed in
the name of Jesus (Hag. 1:6).

Rebuke the devourer for my sake (Mal. 3:11).

All nations will call me blessed, and I will
be a delightful land (Mal. 3:12).

My gates are open continually that the forces (wealth)
of the nations can come into my life (Isa. 60:11).

I am in league with the stones of the field (Job 5:23).

Let Your showers of blessing come upon my life (Ezek. 34:26).

Let my vats overflow (Joel 2:24).

Let my barns be filled with plenty and my
presses burst with new wine (Prov. 3:10).

Command Your blessing upon my storehouse (Deut. 28:8).

Let my barns be full and overflowing. Let my sheep bring forth thousands and ten thousands. Let my oxen be strong to labor (Ps. 144:13–14).

The plowman overtakes the reaper in my life, and the treader of grapes the sower of the seed, and I live in continual harvest (Amos 9:13).

Let my floor be full of wheat and my vats overflow with wine and oil (Joel 2:24).

Deal wondrously with me, and let me eat and be satisfied (Joel 2:26).

Make peace within my border, and fill me with the finest of wheat (Ps. 147:14).

Let me be filled with honey and the finest of wheat (Ps. 81:16).

Lead me into the land flowing with milk and honey (Exod. 3:8).

Bring me into a good land without scarceness and lack (Deut. 8:9).

Make all grace abound toward me, that I will have sufficiency in all things and abound to every good work (2 Cor. 9:8).

Anoint my head with oil, and let my cup run over (Ps. 23:5).

Let me have riches and honor in abundance (2 Chron. 18:1).

Let the rock pour me out rivers of oil (Job 29:6).

Let me dip my feet in oil (Deut. 33:24).

Let me see Your heaps in my life (2 Chron. 31:8).

I love wisdom, I inherit substance, and my treasures are filled (Prov. 8:21).

I receive riches and honor, durable riches and righteousness (Prov. 8:18).

Bring honey out of the rock for me (Ps. 81:16).

Let me eat the finest of wheat (Ps. 147:14).

Let my teeth be white with milk (Gen. 49:12).

Wash my steps with butter (Job 29:6).

Let me lay up gold as dust (Job 22:24).

Let me have plenty of silver (Job 28:1).

Let Your river lead me to gold (Gen. 2:11–12).

Let me inherit the land (Ps. 37:29).

I refuse to allow the angel of blessing to depart without blessing me (Gen. 2:6).

PRAYERS FOR HEALING AND HEALTH

I am healed by the stripes of Jesus (Isa. 53:5).

Jesus carried my sickness and infirmities (Matt. 8:17).

I cast out all spirits of infirmity that would attack my body in the name of Jesus.

I break, rebuke, and cast out any spirit of cancer that would attempt to establish itself in my lungs, bones, breast, throat, back, spine, liver, kidneys, pancreas, skin, or stomach in the name of Jesus.

I rebuke and cast out all spirits causing diabetes, high blood pressure, low blood pressure, heart attack, stroke, kidney failure, leukemia, blood disease, breathing problems, arthritis, lupus, Alzheimer's, or insomnia in the name of Jesus.

I speak healing and strength to my bones, muscles, joints, organs, head, eyes, throat, glands, blood, marrow, lungs, kidneys, liver, spleen, spine, pancreas, eyes, bladder, ears, nose, sinuses, mouth, tongue, and feet in the name of Jesus.

I loose myself from all heart attacks rooted in fear, and I command all spirits of fear to leave in Jesus's name (Luke 21:26).

I loose myself from all diabetes rooted in rejection, self-hatred, inheritance, and guilt, and I command these spirits to come out in the name of Jesus.

I loose myself from all cancer rooted in bitterness, unforgiveness, resentment, and slander of the tongue; and I command these spirits to come out in the name of Jesus.

I loose myself from lupus rooted in self-rejection, self-hatred, and guilt; and I cast these spirits out in the name of Jesus.

I loose myself from all multiple sclerosis rooted in self-hatred, guilt, and rejection from the father; and I cast these spirits out in the name of Jesus.

I loose myself from rheumatoid arthritis that is rooted in self-hatred and low self-esteem, and I command these spirits to come out in the name of Jesus.

I loose myself from high cholesterol that is rooted in anger and hostility and command these spirits to come out in the name of Jesus.

I loose myself from all sinus problems rooted in fear and anxiety, and I command these spirits to come out in the name of Jesus.

I loose myself from all high blood pressure rooted in fear and anxiety, and I command these spirits to come out in the name of Jesus.

I loose myself from asthma rooted in fear concerning relationships in the name of Jesus.

I loose myself from a weakened immune system that is rooted in a broken spirit or broken heart, and I command these spirits to come out in the name of Jesus.

I loose myself from all strokes rooted in self-rejection, self-bitterness, and self-hatred; and I command these spirits to come out in the name of Jesus.

I loose myself from all bone diseases rooted in envy and jealousy, and I command these spirits to come out in the name of Jesus (Prov. 14:30).

Forgive me, Lord, for allowing any fear, guilt, self-rejection, self-hatred, unforgiveness, bitterness, sin, pride, or rebellion to open the door to any sickness or infirmity. I renounce these things in the name of Jesus.

I cast out any spirit of infirmity that came into my life through pride in the name of Jesus.

I cast out any spirit of infirmity that came into my life through trauma or accidents in the name of Jesus.

I cast out any spirit of infirmity that came into my life through rejection in the name of Jesus.

I cast out any spirit of infirmity that came into my life through witchcraft in the name of Jesus.

Give me a sound heart, which is the life of my flesh. Remove from my heart any evil or sinful attitude.

Lord, remove any darts from my liver (Prov. 7:23).

Heal and deliver me from all my pains in the name of Jesus.

I rebuke any sickness that would come to eat up my flesh, including cancer, in the name of Jesus (Ps. 27:2).

Let no evil diseases (things of Belial) cleave to my body (Ps. 41:8).

I break all curses of sickness and disease, and I command all hereditary spirits of sickness to come out (Gal. 3:13).

I break all curses of premature death and destruction in the name of Jesus.

I prosper and walk in health even as my soul prospers (3 John 2).

I receive the Word of God, which is health to my flesh (Prov. 4:22).

Lord, bless my bread and water, and take sickness away from me (Exod. 23:25).

I command every organ in my body to function
the way God intended (Ps. 139:14).

My bones are fat because I receive the good
report of the gospel (Prov. 15:30).

Lord, keep all my bones (Ps. 34:20).

Let every tumor or evil growth melt at
the presence of God (Ps. 97:5).

Let any infection in my body be burned by the fire of God.

I release myself from all allergies and sinus
problems in the name of Jesus.

I pray for my arteries and blood vessels to be opened and my
circulatory system to function properly in the name of Jesus.

I rebuke all fevers in the name of Jesus (Luke 4:39).

My flesh shall be fresher than a child's, and I will
return to the days of my youth (Job 33:25).

I pray for my immune system to be strengthened
in the name of Jesus (Ps. 119:28).

Lord, renew my youth like the eagle's (Ps. 103:5).

I will live and not die, and I will proclaim
the name of the Lord (Ps. 118:17).

My beauty shall be as the olive tree (Hos. 14:6).

Lord, You heal all of my diseases (Ps. 103:3).

Lord, You are the health of my countenance (Ps. 43:5).

Heal me, O Lord, and I shall be healed (Jer. 17:14).

Let Your virtue touch my life and heal me (Luke 6:19).

I release the fire of God to burn out any sickness or disease
that would operate in my body in the name of Jesus.

No sickness or plague will come near my dwelling (Ps. 91:10).

Jesus, arise over my life with healing in Your wings (Mal. 4:2).

The Lord is the strength of my life (Ps. 27:1).

I command every germ or sickness that touches
my body to die in the name of Jesus.

I take the shield of faith and quench every
fiery dart of the enemy (Eph. 6:16).

I am redeemed from sickness and disease (Gal. 3:13).

Every plague is stopped when it comes near me through
the atonement of Jesus Christ (Num. 16:50).

I loose myself from every infirmity (Luke 13:12).

Jesus Christ makes me whole (Acts 9:34).

I am fearfully and wonderfully made. Let my body function in
the wonderful way You designed it to function (Ps. 139:14).

PRAYERS OF DELIVERANCE

Keep my soul, and deliver me (Ps. 25:20).

Be pleased, O Lord, to deliver me (Ps. 40:13).

Make haste, O God, and deliver me (Ps. 70:1).

Deliver me in Your righteousness (Ps. 71:2).

Deliver me, O God, out of the hand of the enemy (Ps. 71:4).

Deliver me from my persecutors (Ps. 142:6).

Deliver me out of great waters (Ps. 144:7).

Deliver me from the oppression of man (Ps. 119:134).

Deliver me according to Your Word (Ps. 119:170).

Deliver my soul from lying lips and a deceitful tongue (Ps. 120:2).

Deliver me from my enemies, and hide me (Ps. 143:9).

Surround me with songs of deliverance (Ps. 32:7).

Command deliverances for my life (Ps. 44:4).

Deliver me from all my fears (Ps. 34:4).

Deliver me out of all my trouble (Ps. 54:7).

Deliver me from them who hate me (Ps. 69:14).

Deliver me out of my distresses (Ps. 107:6).

Send Your Word, and deliver me out of destruction (Ps. 107:20).

Deliver my soul from death, my eyes from tears,
and my feet from falling (Ps. 116:8).

I call upon the name of Jesus, and I am delivered (Joel 2:32).

Deliver me from the power of the lion (Dan. 6:27).

Through Your knowledge I am delivered (Prov. 11:9).

Through Your wisdom I am delivered (Prov. 28:26).

I receive miracles of deliverance for my life (Dan. 6:27).

PRAYERS FOR DELIVERANCE FROM EVIL

Deliver me from evil (Matt. 6:13).

I pray that You would keep me from evil (1 Chron. 4:10).

No evil will touch me (Job 5:19).

Put to shame those who wish me evil (Ps. 40:14).

Let no evil disease cleave to my body (Ps. 41:8).

I will not be afraid of evil tidings (Ps. 112:7).

I will not be visited with evil (Prov. 19:23).

I refrain my feet from every evil way so that I
might keep Your Word (Ps. 119:101).

Preserve me from all evil (Ps. 121:7).

Deliver me from the evil man (Ps. 140:1).

Let people be healed of plagues and evil spirits (Luke 7:21).

I pray that You would keep me from evil (John 17:15).

Let evil spirits be cast out (Acts 19:12).

I will not be overcome with evil, but I
overcome evil with good (Rom. 12:21).

I put on the whole armor of God, that I might
stand in the evil day (Eph. 6:13).

I cancel all the plans and forces of evil sent against my life.

Let the works of evil be burned by Your holy fire.

Let men repent of evil and turn to righteousness.

Let no evil be established in my life, but let
Your righteousness be established.

I loose myself from all evildoers and evil soul ties.

Deliverance and Renunciation of Sexual Sin

I renounce all sexual sin that I have been involved with in
the past, including fornication, masturbation, pornography,
perversion, fantasy, and adultery in the name of Jesus.

I break all curses of adultery, perversion, fornication,
lust, incest, rape, molestation, illegitimacy, harlotry,
and polygamy in the name of Jesus.

I command all spirits of lust and perversion to come
out of my stomach, genitals, eyes, mind, mouth,
hands, and blood in the name of Jesus.

I present my body to the Lord as a living sacrifice (Rom. 12:1).

My members are the members of Christ. I will not let
them be the members of a harlot (1 Cor. 6:15).

I release the fire of God to burn out all unclean
lust from my life in the name of Jesus.

I break all ungodly soul ties with former and sexual partners in the name of Jes

I cast out all spirits of loneliness that would d ungodly sexual relationships in the name of Jesus.

I command all spirits of hereditary lust from my ancestors to come out in the name of Jesus.

I command all spirits of witchcraft that work with lust to leave in the name of Jesus.

I take authority over my thoughts and bind all spirits of fantasy and lustful thinking in the name of Jesus.

I cast out all marriage-breaking spirits of lust that would break covenant in the name of Jesus.

I cast out and loose myself from any spirit spouses and spirits of incubus and succubus in the name of Jesus.

I cast out all spirits of perversion, including Moabite and Ammonite spirits of lust, in the name of Jesus.

I receive the spirit of holiness in my life to walk in sexual purity in the name of Jesus (Rom. 1:4).

I loose myself from the spirit of the world, the lust of the flesh, the lust of the eyes, and the pride of life. I overcome the world through the power of the Holy Spirit (1 John 2:16).

I am crucified with Christ. I mortify my members. I do not let sin reign in my body, and I will not obey its lust (Rom. 6:6–12).

PRAYERS FOR ANGELIC DELIVERANCE

Let Your angels ascend and descend upon my life (Gen. 28:12).

Give Your angels charge over me, and deliver me (Ps. 91:11).

Let the angel of the Lord chase the enemy (Ps. 35:5).

Let the angel of the Lord persecute the enemy (Ps. 35:6).

Let Your angels fight for me in the heavens
against principalities (Dan. 10:13).

Let the angel of Your presence save me (Isa. 63:9).

Let Your angels go before me and make the
crooked places straight (Zech. 12:8).

Send Your angels before me to prosper my way (Exod. 33:2).

Lord, hear my voice and send Your angels to deliver me (Num. 20:16).

Send Your angels to minister unto me (Matt. 4:11).

I have come to Zion and to an innumerable
company of angels (Heb. 12:22).

I am an heir of salvation. Send Your angels
to minister to me (Heb. 1:14).

Send Your angels to deliver me from the
hand of the enemy (Matt. 12:11).

Lord, confess me before Your holy angels (Luke 12:8).

Send Your angels in the night to minister to me (Acts 27:23).

Let Your angels meet me as I walk in my destiny (Gen. 32:1).

Send Your angels to be involved in reaching the lost (Acts 8:26).

Release Your angelic army to fight for and
defend Your church (Ps. 68:17).

Send Your angels to smite the demons that
come to destroy me (Isa. 37:36).

PRAYERS AGAINST TERRORISM

I bind and rebuke every red eagle of terror that would come
against my nation in the name of Jesus (Jer. 49:22).

I will not be afraid of the terror by night (Ps. 91:5).

I bind and rebuke all terrorists that would plot
against my nation in the name of Jesus.

I bind and rebuke all spirits of hatred and murder that would manifest through terrorism in the name of Jesus.

I bind and rebuke all religious terrorists in the name of Jesus.

I bind and rebuke all demons of jihad in the name of Jesus.

I bind and rebuke all spirits of antichrist and hatred of Christianity in the name of Jesus.

I bind all spirits of hatred of America in the name of Jesus.

I bind and rebuke the terrors of death in the name of Jesus (Ps. 55:4).

I bind all fear and panic that would come through terrorism in the name of Jesus.

Deliver me from violent and bloodthirsty men (Ps. 140:1).

I cut the acts of violence out of the hands of the wicked (Isa. 59:6).

Let the assemblies of violent men be exposed and cut off (Ps. 86:14).

Let violence be no more in my borders (Isa. 60:18).

APOSTOLIC PRAYERS

Father, keep me from all evil (John 17:15).

Sanctify me through Your Word of truth (John 17:17).

Let me be one with my brothers and sisters that the world might believe I have been sent (John 17:21).

My heart's desire and prayer for Israel is that they might be saved (Rom. 10:1).

Let me be counted worthy of my calling and fulfill all the good pleasure of Your goodness and the work of faith with power (2 Thess. 1:11).

Let Your Word have free course in my life (2 Thess. 3:1).

Give me the spirit of wisdom and revelation
in the knowledge of Jesus (Eph. 1:17).

Let the eyes of my understanding be enlightened, that I might
know what is the hope of my calling, what are the riches of the
glory of Your inheritance in the saints, and what is the exceeding
greatness of Your power toward me who believes (Eph. 1:17–19).

Strengthen me with might by Your Spirit
in the inner man (Eph. 3:16).

Let Christ dwell in my heart by faith and let me be
rooted and grounded in love and let me comprehend
with all saints what is the breadth and length and
depth and height of Your love (Eph. 3:17–18).

Let me know the love of Christ, which passes all understanding,
that I might be filled with all the fullness of God (Eph. 3:19).

Lord, do exceeding abundantly above all I can ask or think,
according to the power that works in me (Eph. 3:20).

Let utterance be given unto me, that I may open my mouth
boldly to make known the mystery of the gospel (Eph. 6:19).

Let my love abound more and more in knowledge
and in all judgment (Phil. 1:9).

Let me approve things that are excellent, that I might be sincere
and without offense until the day of Christ (Phil. 1:10).

Let me know Jesus and the power of His resurrection
and the fellowship of His sufferings, being made
conformable unto His death (Phil. 3:10).

Let me be filled with the knowledge of Your will in all wisdom
and spiritual understanding, that I might walk worthy of
You unto all pleasing, being fruitful in every good work
and increasing in the knowledge of God (Col. 1:9–10).

Let me be strengthened with all might according to Your glorious power, unto all patience and longsuffering with joyfulness (Col. 1:11).

Let me stand perfect and complete in all the will of God (Col. 4:12).

Let my whole spirit and soul and body be preserved blameless unto the coming of my Lord Jesus Christ (1 Thess. 5:23).

Lord, give me peace always by all means, and be with me (2 Thess. 3:16).

I make supplication, intercession, and give thanks for all men and leaders in my nation and in the church, that I might lead a quiet and peaceable life in all godliness and honesty (1 Tim. 2:1–2).

I receive multiplied grace and peace through the apostolic anointing (2 Pet. 1:2).

BINDING AND LOOSING

I have the keys of the kingdom, and whatever I bind on Earth is bound in heaven, and whatever I loose on Earth is loosed in heaven (Matt. 16:19).

I bind the kings in chains and the nobles with fetters of iron (Ps. 149:8).

I bind the strongman and spoil his goods (Matt. 12:29).

I bind leviathan and all proud spirits arrayed against my life (Job 41:5).

I bind the principalities, powers, rulers of the darkness of this world, and spiritual wickedness in high places (Eph. 6:12).

I bind all sickness and disease released against my mind or body.

Let the exiles be loosed (Isa. 51:14).

Let the prisoners be loosed (Ps. 146:7).

Loose those appointed to death (Ps. 102:20).

I loose my neck from all bands (Isa. 52:2).

I loose myself from the bands of wickedness (Isa. 58:6).

I loose myself from the bands of Orion (Job 38:31).

I loose myself from all bonds (Ps. 116:16).

I loose my mind, will, and emotions from every assignment and spirit of darkness in the name of Jesus.

I loose my city and region from every assignment of hell.

I loose my finances from every spirit of poverty, debt, and lack.

I loose myself from all generational curses and hereditary spirits (Gal. 3:13).

I loose myself from every assignment of witchcraft, sorcery, and divination.

I loose myself from every spoken curse and negative word spoken against my life.

RELEASING SHAME UPON THE ENEMY

Let the enemy be ashamed and sore vexed. Let them return and be ashamed suddenly (Ps. 6:10).

Show me a token for good, that they which hate me may see and be ashamed (Ps. 86:17).

Put to shame those who seek after my soul (Ps. 35:4).

Let those who seek to hurt me be clothed with shame (Ps. 35:26).

Scatter their bones, and put them to shame (Ps. 53:5).

Let those who seek after my soul be ashamed and confounded; let those who desire my hurt be turned backward and put to confusion (Ps. 70:2).

Fill their faces with shame (Ps. 83:16).

Let all those incensed against You be ashamed (Isa. 45:24).

Let those who arise against me be ashamed (Ps. 109:28).

Let the proud spirits be ashamed (Ps. 119:78).

Prayers for Souls

All souls belong to You, O Lord (Ezek. 18:4).

Lord, You are the shepherd and bishop of my soul. Watch over my soul and keep it (1 Pet. 2:25).

I receive with meekness the engrafted word that is able to save my soul (James 1:21).

I bind the hunter of souls (Ezek. 13:20).

In patience I possess my soul (Luke 21:19).

I bind and tear off every veil used to hunt souls and make them fly (Ezek. 13:20).

I command the souls that are hunted by the enemy to be let go (Ezek. 13:20).

I release the souls from divination and witchcraft (Ezek. 13:23).

Return, O Lord, and deliver my soul (Ps. 6:4).

Let not the enemy persecute my soul (Ps. 7:5).

Lord, restore my soul (Ps. 23:3).

Keep my soul, and deliver me (Ps. 25:20).

Put to shame those who seek after my soul (Ps. 35:4).

Rescue my soul from destruction (Ps. 35:17).

Let those who seek after my soul be ashamed and confounded (Ps. 40:14).

Deliver me from all oppressors who seek after my soul (Ps. 54:3).

Lord, You have delivered my soul from death and my feet from falling (Ps. 56:13).

Preserve my soul, for I am holy (Ps. 86:2).

Rejoice, my soul, for I lift up my soul unto You (Ps. 86:4).

Lord, Your comforts delight my soul (Ps. 94:19).

I break the power of all negative words
spoken against my soul (Ps. 109:20).

Return unto your rest, O my soul (Ps. 116:7).

My soul shall live and praise the Lord (Ps. 119:175).

My soul is escaped as a bird out of the
snare of the fowler (Ps. 124:7).

Strengthen me with strength in my soul (Ps. 138:3).

Destroy all who afflict my soul (Ps. 143:12).

Let Your fear come upon every soul in my city (Acts 2:43).

I will prosper and be in health, even as my soul prospers (3 John 2).

I pray my soul will be preserved blameless unto
the coming of the Lord (1 Thess. 5:23).

Satiate my soul with fatness (Jer. 31:14).

My soul will be joyful in the Lord. You have covered me with the
garments of salvation and the robe of righteousness (Isa. 61:10).

I break all ungodly soul ties and pray for godly soul ties
that will bring blessing to my life (1 Sam. 18:1).

I loose my soul from any oaths, inner vows, and
curses that would bind it in the name of Jesus.

PRAYERS FOR YOUR NATION

I pray for the leaders of my nation to come to the light (Isa. 60:3).

I make supplication, prayer, intercession, and give
thanks for all the people of my nation and for the
leaders of my nation, that I might live a peaceable
life in all godliness and honesty (1 Tim. 2:1–2).

Let our leaders be just, and let them rule by
the fear of the Lord (2 Sam. 23:3).

Let our leaders fall down before the Lord, and
let my nation serve Him (Ps. 72:11).

Let the poor and needy people of my nation
be delivered (Ps. 72:12–13).

Let the Lord's dominion be established in my nation,
and let His enemies lick the dust (Ps. 72:8–9).

Turn our leaders' hearts to fear You (Prov. 21:1)

Let the Lord rule over my nation, and let my
nation be glad and rejoice (Ps. 97:1).

Let my nation sing a new song, bless His name, and show
forth His salvation from day to day (Ps. 96:1–3).

Let the people of my nation tremble at the
presence of the Lord (Ps. 99:1).

Let my nation make a joyful noise to the Lord, and let
the people serve Him with gladness (Ps. 110:1–2).

Let our leaders praise You, and let them hear
the words of Your mouth (Ps. 138:4).

Let the wicked be rooted out of our land (Prov. 2:22).

Let the wicked be cut down and wither
as the green herb (Ps. 37:2).

Let all the people of my nation turn to the
Lord and worship Him (Ps. 22:27).

My nation is the Lord's and the fullness thereof,
and all they that dwell therein (Ps. 24:1).

Let all the idolaters in my nation be confounded, and
let all the gods worship the Lord (Ps. 97:7).

Let my nation praise the Lord for His merciful
kindness and truth (Ps. 117).

Save my nation, O Lord, and send prosperity (Ps. 118:25).

I pray that my nation will submit to the rule
and reign of Christ (Dan. 7:14).

I pray my nation will bring its wealth
into the kingdom (Rev. 21:24).

I pray my nation will be converted and bring
its wealth to the king (Isa. 60:5).

I pray my nation will be healed by the leaves
from the tree of life (Rev. 22:2).

I pray my nation will show forth the praises of God (Isa. 60:6).

I pray my nation will see the glory of God (Isa. 35:2).

Let those who are deaf hear the words of the book,
and let the blind see out of obscurity (Isa. 29:18).

I pray that Jesus will rule over my nation in
righteousness and judgment (Isa. 32:1).

I pray my nation will come to Zion to be taught,
and learn war no more (Isa. 2:1–4).

I pray that my nation will seek the Lord
and enter into His rest (Isa. 11:1).

I pray that the parched places in my nation will become a
pool, and every thirsty part springs of water (Isa. 35:7).

I pray that the glory of the Lord be revealed to my nation,
and that all the inhabitants will see it (Isa. 40:5).

Let the Lord bring righteousness and
judgment to my nation (Isa. 42:1).

I ask the Lord to do a new thing in my nation by giving waters
in the wilderness and streams in the desert (Isa. 43:19–20).

Let peace (*shalom*) come into my nation like a river (Isa. 66:12).

Let my nation be sprinkled by the blood of Jesus (Isa. 52:12).

Let the children of my nation be taught of the Lord (Isa. 54:13).

I pray that my nation will seek and find the Lord (Isa. 65:1).

Let my nation be filled with priests and Levites
that worship the Lord (Isa. 66:21).

Let the people of my nation come and
worship the Lord (Isa. 66:23).

Let my people build houses and inhabit them (Isa. 65:21).

Let my people plant vineyards and eat
the fruit of them (Isa. 65:21).

Let my people long enjoy the work of their hands (Isa. 65:22).

Let the enemies in my land be reconciled (Isa. 65:25).

Let my nation be filled with the knowledge
of the glory of the Lord (Hab. 2:14).

Let my nation be saved and walk in the light of Zion (Rev. 21:24).

Let God be merciful unto us and bless us, and cause
His face to shine upon us. Let His way be known to us,
and His saving health in our nation (Ps. 67:1–2).

Let every covenant with death and hell be
broken in our nation (Isa. 28:18).

Let my nation look to the Lord and be saved (Isa. 45:22).

Let the Lord make bare His holy arm, and let my
nation see the salvation of the Lord (Isa. 52:10).

Let every veil spread over my nation be destroyed (Isa. 25:7).

My nation is the inheritance of the Lord;
let Him possess it (Ps. 2:7–8).

The kingdom is the Lord's, and He is the
governor of my nation (Ps. 22:28).

Let the people who walk in darkness in my nation
see the light, and let Your light shine upon those
in the shadow of darkness (Isa. 9:2).

Let His government and peace (shalom)
continually increase in my nation (Isa. 9:7).

Let His justice and judgment increase in my nation (Isa. 9:7).

Let those in my nation who were not Your people be
called the children of the living God (Rom. 9:25–26).

Let righteousness, peace, and joy in the Holy
Ghost increase in my nation (Rom. 14:17).

I pray for righteousness to come to my nation, and
that my nation would be exalted (Prov. 14:34).

Let His Spirit be poured out in my nation, and let our
sons and daughters prophesy (Acts 2:17–18).

I will confess You, Lord, among my people
and sing unto Your name (Ps. 22:22).

Let Your glory be declared among my people, and
Your wonders in my nation (Ps. 96:20).

Open a door of utterance in my nation, that my
people might hear Your Word (Col. 4:3).

I pray that the families of my people be blessed
through Christ (Gen. 28:14, Gal. 3:14).

I pray for the healing waters to flow into my nation (Ezek. 47:9).

BOOK 2

PRAYERS THAT BREAK CURSES

JOHN ECKHARDT

CHARISMA
HOUSE

Contents

INTRODUCTION

REDEEMED FROM the CURSE OF BELIAL

Do FAILURE AND frustration seem to be your lot in life? Is your life characterized by continual setbacks and misfortune? Does it appear as though no matter what you do in life, you cannot seem to obtain the blessings of the Lord?

Often the most frustrating thing about this whole scenario is the fact that you are a believer and love the Lord. According to Galatians 3:13, we are redeemed from the curse. In other words, Jesus became a curse in our stead. If this is true, then how can a believer still be under a curse?

Unfortunately, there are still many believers living under curses even though they have been legally redeemed from curses. Just as a believer may have to fight a good fight of faith for healing, he or she may also have to fight a good fight of faith against curses.

Many of the curses that can affect a person's life come as a result of one of the most wicked and vile spirits in the kingdom of darkness—the spirit of *Belial*.

He is a *ruling* spirit of *wickedness*. There is a host of demons that operate under his command, cursing the lives of people, which we will discuss in this book. Belial is mentioned twenty-seven times in the Old Testament and once in the New Testament. It is from the Hebrew word *beliyaal*, which is translated as "Belial" sixteen times in the Old Testament.

This word is also translated in other verses as "wicked," "ungodly," and "naughty." *Strong's* definition of *beliyaal* is "without profit, worthlessness, destruction, wickedness, evil, naughty." The most common of these definitions is "worthlessness."

Webster's definition of *worthless* is "valueless, useless, contemptible, despicable." *Despicable* is defined as "deserving to be despised: so worthless or obnoxious as to rouse moral indignation."

Therefore, *Belial's work* is to curse men and women, causing them to commit sins that are vile and contemptible. All sin is wrong, and I don't make any excuses or allowances for any sin. However, there are some sins more abominable than others. That is, there are different *degrees* of sin.

Under the Law, there were some sins that were considered abominations and punishable by death, while other sins required certain sacrifices. Belial's work is to draw a nation into such abominable sins that it will bring the curse and the judgment of God.

When I observe the practices and sins that are happening in our nation today, I know that the spirit of Belial is behind them. Belial is a strongman in America as well as other nations of the world. Belial is a world ruler of wickedness. Jesus taught us the necessity of binding the strongman in order to spoil his goods (Matt. 12:29). The prayers in this book are meant to do just that—as you pray, Belial, the world ruler of wickedness, will be bound, and his demonic hold on you and on your family and community will be broken.

CHAPTER 1

CURSES CAUSED by the SPIRIT of IDOLATRY

Certain men, the children of Belial, are gone out from among you, and have withdrawn the inhabitants of their city, saying, Let us go and serve other gods, which ye have not known.
—Deuteronomy 13:13

THIS VERSE IS the first mention of Belial in the Word of God. The Lord identifies men who attempt to lead His people *away from Him* to serve other gods as "children of Belial" in the King James Version. This passage of Scripture goes on to describe their actions:

> If you hear someone in one of your cities, which the LORD your God gives you to dwell in, saying, "Corrupt men have gone out from among you and enticed the inhabitants of their city, saying, 'Let us go and serve other gods'"—which you have not known—then you shall inquire, search out, and ask

5

diligently. And if it is indeed true and certain that such an abomination was committed among you, you shall surely strike the inhabitants of that city with the edge of the sword, utterly destroying it, all that is in it and its livestock, with the edge of the sword. And you shall gather all its plunder into the middle of the street, and completely burn with fire the city and all its plunder, for the LORD your God; and it shall be a heap forever. It shall not be built again. So none of the accursed things shall remain in your hand, that the LORD may turn from the fierceness of His anger and show you mercy, have compassion on you and multiply you, just as He swore to your fathers.

—Deuteronomy 13:12–17

"Children of Belial" indicates individuals who were under the control of Belial. They were being used by Belial to draw the people of God away from Him to serve other gods. It is interesting to note that the word *idol* is the Hebrew word *eliyl*, which means "good for nothing, vain or vanity, of no value, thing of nought." This can be summed up in one word—*worthless*.

Belial, which means "worthlessness," tries to lead men astray to follow something that is worthless. Idols are worthless; they have no value, and they cannot satisfy. There is a principle of Bible study that we call the law of first reference. This law of Bible study says that whenever a subject or a particular word is *first mentioned* in the Bible, there are some important principles that will be found concerning that subject or word.

The *first principle* we see in connection with Belial is that he attempts to draw people away from worshiping the true God. Under Belial are spirits that will *seduce* people and draw them away from the Lord. As a result, the demon spirits operating under the rulership of Belial inflict the people who have been drawn away from the protection of God with bondages and curses that often lead to destruction.

The apostle Paul prophesied, "In the latter times some shall depart from the faith, giving heed to seducing spirits, and doctrines of devils" (1 Tim. 4:1). *To seduce* means "to lead away, to persuade to disobedience or disloyalty, to lead astray by persuasion or false promises, to attract, to lure." The Living Bible translation of this verse says, "Some in the church will turn away from Christ." This is known as *apostasy*.

Webster's defines *apostasy* as "abandonment of a previous loyalty, defection." I believe this is the reason why so many churches and some denominations have abandoned the faith. Some have even ordained homosexuals as ministers. What an abomination! This is no doubt the work of Belial and seducing spirits to cause many to *apostatize*.

PRAYERS

CHARACTERISTICS OF THE SPIRIT OF BELIAL

Father, Your Word tells me, "Some worthless people have talked everyone there into worshiping other gods, even though these gods had never done anything for them." You instruct me to "carefully find out if the rumor is true" and call such action "a disgusting thing" (Deut. 13:13–14, CEV). Make me a watchman on the wall to guard against this worthless spirit leading those I know and love astray.

Father, the spirit of Belial causes people "to be so selfish that you refuse to help the poor" (Deut. 15:9, CEV)—even when the poor are their own relatives! You warn me not to be like that and say that if that person I refuse to help tells You of the wrong I do, You "will say that [I am] guilty." Protect me from the spirit of Belial, who makes people so selfish.

God, the spirit of Belial is so perverted that it watches for strangers to visit Your people and then demands that the stranger be given to perverse men and women to satisfy their homosexual lust (Judg. 19:22, NKJV). Keep me ever watchful, Lord, for those who would be stolen away by the homosexual lusts of Belial. Make me a strong wall of protection and my home a locked fortress against this spirit.

Your Word tells the horrible story of a traveling Levite who, with his wife, spent a night in the home of a fellow Jew who lived in a city filled with men who were no longer living for God but were filled with the spirit of Belial. These men surrounded the man's home and demanded that the Levite be given to them for homosexual relations. Rather than protecting his wife, this Levite threw his own wife out the door, and she was repeatedly raped by these evil men and died. (See Judges 19.) Lord, teach me to heed the warning of this story and never become so apathetic toward You that I would willingly give up my own family members to evil. Keep me safe in the protection of Your will so that I never stray from You and fall victim or allow my loved ones to fall victim to the spirit of Belial.

Lord, when Hannah was interceding in the temple for a son, she was thought to be a daughter of Belial who was drunk (1 Sam. 1:12–16, NKJV). Help me to recognize that the spirit of Belial would attempt to bring me under the bondage of some addictive sin that traps me. Help me to recognize these addictive bondages and to avoid anything that could draw me subtly into bondage.

Father, You called the sons of Eli—priests in Your temple—sons of Belial who were living in sin even as they pretended to be men of God (1 Sam. 2:12). Protect the men and women who have accepted Your calling to ministry, and shield them from the hidden sins that will lead them away from You. Break the power of sin from their lives, and keep them true and honorable shepherds who lead Your people into righteousness.

Father, like Eli's sons, so many church leaders and men of God today have fallen prey to the spirit of Belial and have ended up broken, bound by sin, and unworthy to serve as Your shepherds. Help me to pray and intercede for Your shepherds. Break the power of Belial to lead Your servants astray. Keep them pure and holy and blameless before God and before the people they are leading.

Father, as soon as Samuel had anointed Saul to be king, the spirit of Belial immediately attacked him by casting doubts to the people about his ability to lead them and by their refusing to honor him with their gifts (1 Sam. 10:27, NKJV). The spirit of Belial was already at work, filling Saul with self-doubt and insecurities about his abilities. Even though he held his peace, this spirit began its insidious attack against him, ultimately leading him to reject You and fail miserably at the job You had called him to.

Make me strong against Belial when it tempts me to doubt what You have called me to do or tempts me to feel inadequate or inept. Make me powerful through Your Spirit, and defeat the spirit of Belial from my life.

God, when King David asked the rich man Nabal to share some food with him and his men as they were passing nearby, Nabal was so filled with the spirit of Belial that he refused to give David any food. Even though David and his men had always treated the servants of Nabal kindly and with respect, Nabal sent a rude message back to David, saying, "What makes you think I would take my bread, my water, and the meat that I've had cooked for my own servants and give it to you?" (1 Sam. 25:11, CEV). Lord, may I never become like Nabal! Give me a generous heart and a spirit filled with Your mercy and compassion. Break the power of Belial from turning me into a Nabal.

Father, even Nabal's own wife, Abigail, recognized how sinfully bound he was by the spirit of Belial. She generously fed David and his men and apologized for her evil husband, saying, "Sir, please let me explain! Don't pay any attention to that good-for-nothing Nabal. His name means 'fool,' and it really fits him!" (1 Sam. 25:24–25, CEV). May I never be identified as a fool or a son or daughter of Belial.

Protect me from sinful selfishness and stinginess. Allow me to be an Abigal, not a Nabal, in the way I treat others.

Lord, Your Word teaches that the spirit of Belial can creep in among believers and bind them to sinfulness and evil desires. Even some of David's men were servants of Belial, and David had to rebuke them for being greedy and unwilling to share with those less fortunate than them (1 Sam. 30:22, NKJV). Reveal any greediness or selfishness in my heart, and break the spirit of Belial from out of my life.

Father, we learn from the example of Shimei that the spirit of Belial will cause us to accuse others of the very sins we have in our own lives. Shimei, one of Saul's relatives, blamed David for the death of Saul and accused him of stealing the kingdom. This man was so possessed by the spirit of Belial that he could not see Your plan and David's commitment to Your plan (2 Sam. 16:7, NKJV). Father, keep me from being blinded by the spirit of Belial. Reveal my own sinfulness and evil, and keep me from accusing Your children of the ungodly evil tendencies at work in my own life.

Father, Your Word teaches us to deal firmly and permanently with another believer who allows the spirit of Belial to cause him to lead in a rebellion against Your servants. When David recognized that a member of the tribe of Benjamin was inciting a rebellion against him, he took action. He knew that evil spirit could break down the protective spiritual walls around other believers' lives and cause them to fall into evil with Sheba. He pulled his army together and chased after Sheba until he found him and made sure he had been defeated and killed. (See 2 Samuel 20.) Give me the courage to curse the spirit of Belial and destroy it from my life and from the lives of other believers so it cannot tear down the protective spiritual walls around our hearts and lead us into evil.

Father, David recognized that the evil flooding out from the spirit of Belial can cause us to be afraid and swallow us up in the flood of evil (2 Sam. 22:5, NKJV). When I am afraid and in the midst of "terrible trouble," help me to be like David and to call out to You for help. Protect me from the overwhelming floods of Belial.

Father, help me to recognize the power of Belial and to arm myself with the sword of Your Spirit to fight this evil spirit. It cannot be "pulled up like thornbushes," or "dug up by hand." It requires "a sharp spear" to destroy it and must be "burned on the spot" (2 Sam. 23:6–7, CEV). Keep me from trying to find evil in my own strength. Arm me with Your Spirit and strength, and burn evil from my life.

The spirit of Belial is a lying spirit that accuses Your children and carries out evil plots against them to destroy them and steal everything that belongs to them. This is revealed in the story of Ahab and Jezebel's plot against Naboth (1 Kings 21). Make me a fearless, courageous servant like Elijah, who was not afraid to confront these evil servants of Belial and to forecast their judgment from God to a horrible death.

Father, when evil Jeroboam and his followers set out to destroy the righteous followers of God, Abijah, king of Judah, confronted him and declared, "God is on our side.... You might as well give up. There's no way you can defeat the LORD" (2 Chron. 13:12, CEV). With God's help, Abijah defeated Jeroboam and the people of Israel who had rebelled against God to become servants of Belial. When Your people today rebel against You and begin to serve Belial, raise up Abijahs who will stand for righteousness and godliness in the midst of apathy and evil. Make me an Abijah, and arm me for the battle for righteousness in America.

Lord, in times of illness and physical distress, keep my eyes focused on You and my heart strong in my faith that You can heal me. The spirit of Belial would try to tell me, "You have some fatal disease! You'll never get well" (Ps. 41:8, CEV). Help me to reject the voice of Belial that would whisper defeat, destruction, and death in my ear. Raise me up to strength and physical wholeness by Your power, and block the tauntings of Belial from my ears.

Lord, "I refuse to be corrupt or to take part in anything crooked." I will not allow the spirit of Belial to take control of my life, and "I won't be dishonest or deceitful" (Ps. 101:3–4, CEV). I will live my life in purity and honor. I will listen only to Your Spirit and will resist the spirit of Belial from entering my life.

Lord, worthless liars who have been bound by Belial go around deceiving others (Prov. 6:12, NKJV). I will not be one of these worthless liars. I will speak only Your truth, and I will only seek to lead others into the path of righteousness.

Lord, the spirit of Belial destroys the godly value You have given us and causes us to become worthless. Your Word says, "Worthless people plan trouble. Even their words burn like a flaming fire" (Prov. 16:27, CEV). May I never become worthless to You. May I never play with the fire of Belial and become burned by evil. I will not allow the spirit of Belial to destroy my value to You and to others.

Father, Your Word says, "A lying witness makes

fun of the court system, and criminals think crime is really delicious" (Prov. 19:28, CEV). Help me to recognize the lying witnesses in America today who mock the godly principles this nation was founded on and attempt to convince others that ungodliness is right. Unmask the spirit of Belial in the voices of those who lobby for ungodly practices and rules, who attempt to water down the righteous principles of this nation and lead us into sinful acts and behaviors. Right the wrongs that have crept into our justice system, into our schools and government, and that are attempting to lead this nation into sinful practices.

Lord, Your Word says that the evil plans a wicked servant of Belial makes against You or Your children are doomed, no matter how strong that evil plan is (Nah. 1:11, NKJV). I am to keep my eyes on You and not to be fearful of the evil plans of Belial. I will not fear Belial—even when his plans seem too strong to overcome. I will defeat evil through Your power and in the strength of Your Spirit.

God, Your Word says plainly that people who are not Your followers have nothing in common with people who do follow You. You instruct me, "Leave them and stay away! Don't touch anything that isn't clean. Then I will welcome you and be your Father. You will be my sons and my daughters, as surely as

I am God, the All-Powerful" (2 Cor. 6:17–18, CEV). I commit myself to You, Lord. I welcome You as my Father. I will not touch the filthy evil of Belial. I will live only for You for all the days of my life.

CHAPTER 2

Tꞕe CURSE FROM +ꞕe SEDUCTION Of JEZEBEL

Nevertheless I have a few things against you, because you allow that woman Jezebel, who calls herself a prophetess, to teach and seduce My servants to commit sexual immorality and eat things sacrificed to idols.
—Revelation 2:20, NKJV

BELIAL WORKS WITH *the spirit of Jezebel* to seduce the servants of the Lord into fornication and idolatry. Jezebel can manifest through false teachings and is a seducing spirit.

Again, the intent is to draw people away from the truth and cause them to go into error, causing bondage and curses and bringing upon them the judgment of God.

> Indeed I will cast her into a sickbed, and those who commit adultery with her into great tribulation, unless they repent of their deeds. I will kill her children with death, and all the churches shall know that I am

> He who searches the minds and hearts. And I will
> give to each one of you according to your works.
> —Revelation 2:22–23, NKJV

This was the judgment of the Lord upon those who allowed themselves to be seduced by the teachings of Jezebel. Fornication and adultery will always be judged by the Lord.

> Marriage is honorable among all, and the bed unde-
> filed; but fornicators and adulterers God will judge.
> —Hebrews 13:4, NKJV

Marriage is under attack in America like never before. Divorce is no longer considered unacceptable—it is almost expected. Jezebel is a seducing spirit that draws people into *whoredom* and *adultery*. This will bring the judgment of God.

Whoredom means "prostitution." It also means "faithless, unworthy, or idolatrous practices or pursuits." To *whore* means "a faithless, unworthy, or idolatrous desire, to debauch." Recently, a visiting minister was ministering in our church and began to prophetically identify spirits operating in our region. As he was prophesying, he mentioned in the prophecy the spirit of debauchery. I took note, and the word *debauchery* stayed with me months after the meeting.

I knew that the Lord, through this prophet, was identifying a spirit we had to bind in our region. *To debauch* means "to seduce from chastity, to lead away from virtue or excellence, to corrupt by intemperance or sensuality."

There you have it. Spirits of whoredom, prostitution, and debauchery work under the strongman Belial. *Debauchery* is defined as "extreme indulgence in sensuality." *To be sensual* means "to be fleshly or carnal, deficient in moral, spiritual, or intellectual interests: irreligious."

It is interesting to note that the only reference to Belial in the New Testament is found in 2 Corinthians 6:15: "What concord hath Christ with Belial? or what part hath he that believeth with an infidel?" Paul was dealing with the rampant carnality in the church of Corinth.

Jezebel does not work alone. Belial works with Jezebel to draw people into abominable sins, including sodomy, homosexuality, incest, rape, and perversion of all kinds. Jezebel works through both *manipulation* and *intimidation*. If the spirit of Jezebel cannot manipulate people into sin, then intimation will manifest. Jezebel threatened the prophet Elijah with death. Jezebel hates true apostles and prophets of God.

The greatest threat to Jezebel's influence has always been true servants of God. Those who preach the truth and maintain a standard of holiness are obstacles to the work of Jezebel. This spirit therefore attacks these men and women of God in order to move them out of the way.

PRAYERS

Lord, Your Word teaches that the spirit of Jezebel can masquerade as a person with prophetic giftings and can, therefore, teach and mislead believers to act immorally (Rev. 2:20, NKJV). Reveal Your true prophets and prophetesses, Lord. Keep Your children from being led into sin by someone who masquerades as a messenger from You.

Father, the spirit of Jezebel is a seducing spirit that is causing rampant destruction in America today. Teach me to "honor marriage, and guard the sacredness of sexual intimacy between wife and husband." May I never forget that "God draws a firm line against casual and illicit sex" (Heb. 13:4, THE MESSAGE).

Father, Your Word teaches the painful lesson of the evil influence of Jezebel. Although King Jehoshaphat loved and served You throughout his life, his son Jehoram, who became king after him, married the daughter of wicked Queen Jezebel. Jehoram was influenced by this evil generational spirit and led his kingdom into worshiping false gods and falling into gross immorality in their lives (2 Chron. 21:11). As a result, You caused him to die of a painful stomach disease. Lord, help us to lead our children into godly marriages and to teach them the consequences of becoming unequally yoked in marriage with the evil spirit of Jezebel at work in a person's life.

Lord, Your children were so influenced by the evil spirit of Jezebel in their king's life that they sinned by committing sexual immorality and engaging in fornication (2 Chron. 21:11, NKJV). America has fallen prey to this wicked spirit, and our nation is filled with people who no longer live in purity. Cause Your people to make a stand for purity, Lord. Let Your people lead this nation to repentance for its immorality and to turn to You in purity and dedication.

Father, the spirit of Jezebel drives men and women to commit sinful sexual acts because this spirit cannot be satisfied, and it fills men and women with an insatiable appetite for sex. (See Ezekiel 16:23–31.) This sinful spirit has caused brothels to be built where unspeakable evil takes place. It has created the rise of promiscuity in our youth, paid the sinful price of prostitution, and paved the road to homosexuality. In the holy name of God, I bind this spirit and cast it away from this nation. Break the hold of Jezebel from off me, Lord. Loose the captives, and turn me back to purity.

Father, You teach in Your Word, "'Whoever divorces his wife, let him give her a certificate of divorce.' But I say to you that whoever divorces his wife for any reason except sexual immorality causes her to commit adultery; and whoever marries a woman who is divorced commits adultery" (Matt. 5:31–32, NKJV). Stop the evil influence of Belial at work in America causing men and women to engage in adulterous relationships and sexual immorality. Belial seeks the destruction of Your divine institution of marriage. Keep me pure in my relationships, and let me join the fight to save marriage in America.

Father, help me to understand that "those things which proceed out of the mouth come from the heart, and they defile a man. For out of the heart proceed evil thoughts, murders, adulteries, fornications, thefts, false witness, blasphemies" (Matt. 15:18–19, NKJV). Turn my heart toward You, and keep my mouth pure.

Father, teach me the importance of renewing my mind (Rom. 12:2) and of keeping it focused on You. Your Word tells us of those who "did not like to retain God in their knowledge, God gave them over to a debased mind, to do those things which are not fitting; being filled with all unrighteousness, sexual immorality, wickedness, covetousness, maliciousness; full of envy, murder, strife, deceit, evil-mindedness; they are whisperers, backbiters, haters of God, violent, proud, boasters, inventors of evil things, disobedient to parents" (Rom. 1:28–30, NKJV). I do not want to be like that.

Lord, I know that "the works of the flesh are evident, which are: adultery, fornication, uncleanness, lewdness, idolatry, sorcery, hatred, contentions, jealousies, outbursts of wrath, selfish ambitions, dissensions, heresies" (Gal. 5:19–20, NKJV). Teach me to live by the power of Your Spirit and to destroy the works of the flesh out of my life.

Lord, You give meaning to my life, and I want to live with You in glory. Help me to follow Your instructions: "Don't be controlled by your body. Kill every desire for the wrong kind of sex. Don't be immoral or indecent or have evil thoughts. Don't be greedy, which is the same as worshiping idols" (Col. 3:5, CEV).

Father, "This is the will of God, even your sanctification, that ye should abstain from fornication" (1 Thess. 4:3). Sanctify me fully, Lord, and let me be totally separated unto You so that evil will not creep into my life.

Father, You wrote to the church at Thyatira, "I know everything about you, including your love, your faith, your service, and how you have endured. I know that you are doing more now than you have ever done before. But I still have something against you because of that woman Jezebel. She calls herself a prophet, and you let her teach and mislead my servants to do immoral things and to eat food offered to idols. I gave her a chance to turn from her sins, but she did not want to stop doing these immoral things. I am going to strike down Jezebel. Everyone who does these immoral things with her will also be punished, if they don't stop" (Rev. 2:19–22, CEV). Examine my heart, Lord, and show me my heart. If the spirit of Jezebel is present in my life, I repent, and I plead for Your forgiveness. And if that evil spirit has somehow crept into my family and influenced my family members with her evil teachings, reveal that to me, and cast it out of my home. I want my love for You and my family's love for You to be pure and holy in Your sight.

CHAPTER 3

THE CURSE OF A SEARED CONSCIENCE

And she wrote in the letters, saying, Proclaim a fast, and set Naboth on high among the people: and set two men, sons of Belial, before him, to bear witness against him, saying, Thou didst blaspheme God and the king. And then carry him out, and stone him, that he may die....And there came in two men, children of Belial, and sat before him: and the men of Belial witnessed against him, even against Naboth, in the presence of the people, saying, Naboth did blaspheme God and the king. Then they carried him forth out of the city, and stoned him with stones, that he died. Then they sent to Jezebel, saying, Naboth is stoned, and is dead.
—1 Kings 21:9–10, 13–14

HERE IS AN example of Jezebel and Belial working together. The men of Belial were evidently hired to bear false witness against Naboth. The Living Bible translation says, "Then two men who had no conscience accused him" (v. 13). *Belial causes men to act without conscience.*

Paul further states that there would be those who would be "speaking lies in hypocrisy, having their own conscience seared with a hot iron" (1 Tim. 4:2, NKJV). The Phillips translation says, "…whose consciences are as dead as seared flesh." The Amplified Bible says, "…whose consciences are seared (cauterized)."

To cauterize means "to deaden." One of the ways Belial is able to cause men to commit vile acts is by cauterizing the conscience. Men without a conscience are capable of committing any act without feeling remorse.

Every person is born with a conscience. The enemy must neutralize the conscience before seducing men to commit certain sins. According to Titus 1:15, the mind and conscience can be defiled. *To defile* means "to contaminate or make unclean." This is obviously a reference to evil spirits operating in the conscience.

When the conscience is seared, men and women are opened to all kinds of unclean spirits and their curses and are capable of all kinds of unclean acts. For example, there are many today who no longer feel that homosexuality, lesbianism, and incest are wrong.

Belial has cauterized the conscience to accept these things as acceptable lifestyles. When the conscience has been seared, men are capable of the vilest and most sickening acts. There is almost no limit to the depravity that men can exhibit when they are bound by the curse of a seared conscience.

PRAYERS

Father, like the men who stood ready to stone the woman caught in the act of adultery but who were "convicted by their conscience" and, therefore, "went out one by one, beginning with the oldest even to the last," leaving "Jesus...alone, and the woman standing in the midst" (John 8:9–10, NKJV), convict me of the sins I try to hide and fail to admit, and bring me to repentance.

Father, let me become like Paul, who "earnestly beholding the council, said, Men and brethren, I have lived in all good conscience before God until this day" (Acts 23:1–3).

Lord, "I am just as sure as these people are that God will raise from death everyone who is good or evil. And because I am sure, I try my best to have a clear conscience in whatever I do for God or for people" (Acts 24:15–16, CEV).

Father, as a believer, I know, "We have only one God, and he is the Father. He created everything, and we live for him. Jesus Christ is our only Lord. Everything was made by him, and by him life was given to us." But like the apostle Paul, who wrote, "Not everyone knows these things. In fact, many people have grown up with the belief that idols have life in them. So when they eat meat offered to idols, they are bothered by a weak conscience" (1 Cor. 8:6–7, CEV), make me sensitive to others whose consciences are weak and who may still be bound by ritualistic traditions.

Father, Your Word advises me to "be careful, however, that the exercise of your freedom does not become a stumbling block to the weak" (1 Cor. 8:9, NIV). Keep me sensitive to others so that someone else does not get wounded by my actions, for "when you sin against your brothers in this way and wound their weak conscience, you sin against Christ" (v. 12).

Lord, make me worthy of saying, as Paul did, "Our conscience testifies that we have conducted ourselves in the world, and especially in our relations with you, in the holiness and sincerity that are from God. We have done so not according to worldly wisdom but according to God's grace" (2 Cor. 1:12, NIV).

Father, I renounce "secret and shameful ways" (2 Cor. 4:2, NIV). With Paul, I say, "We use no hocus-pocus, no clever tricks, no dishonest manipulation of the Word of God. We speak the plain truth and so commend ourselves to every man's conscience in the sight of God. If our Gospel is 'veiled,' the veil must be in the minds of those who are spiritually dying" (2 Cor. 4:2–3, PHILLIPS).

Lord, keep me from a seared conscience. Let me serve You in honesty and integrity. Like Paul, "since, then, we know what it is to fear the Lord, we try to persuade men. What we are is plain to God, and I hope it is also plain to your conscience" (2 Cor. 5:11, NIV).

Father, make me the kind of teacher of Your Word that Paul instructed Timothy to be: "Command certain men not to teach false doctrines any longer nor to devote themselves to myths and endless genealogies. These promote controversies rather than God's work—which is by faith. The goal of this command is love, which comes from a pure heart and a good conscience and a sincere faith. Some have wandered away from these and turned to meaningless talk. They want to be teachers of the law, but they do not know what they are talking about or what they so confidently affirm" (1 Tim. 1:3–7, NIV). May everything I do come from "love...a pure heart and a good conscience and a sincere faith" (v. 5).

Lord, let me "fight the good fight, holding on to faith and a good conscience" (1 Tim. 1:18–19, NIV).

Father, only if I keep my life pure and protect my conscience from being seared by sin will I be worthy of serving You as a deacon in Your church. If I am given the sacred trust of a deacon, may I follow Paul's instruction: "Deacons, likewise, are to be men worthy of respect, sincere, not indulging in much wine, and not pursuing dishonest gain. They must keep hold of the deep truths of the faith with a clear conscience. They must first be tested; and then if there is nothing against them, let them serve as deacons" (1 Tim. 3:8–10, NIV).

Father, let me say with Paul, "I thank God, whom I serve, as my forefathers did, with a clear conscience" (2 Tim. 1:3, NIV).

Lord, when we come before You, "let us draw near to God with a sincere heart in full assurance of faith, having our hearts sprinkled to cleanse us from a guilty conscience and having our bodies washed with pure water" (Heb. 10:22, NIV).

Lord, help me to call upon the power of intercessors by asking Your prayer warriors to "keep praying for us, for we are convinced that we have a good (clear) conscience, that we want to walk uprightly and live a noble life, acting honorably and in complete honesty in all things" (Heb. 13:18, AMP).

Lord, give me a conscience that is always following in Your footsteps and remembering how You suffered for me. Your Word reminds me, "For it is commendable if a man bears up under the pain of unjust suffering because he is conscious of God. But how is it to your credit if you receive a beating for doing wrong and endure it? But if you suffer for doing good and you endure it, this is commendable before God" (1 Pet. 2:19–20, NIV).

Father, I want to be the kind of Christian who can follow the advice of Paul: "Honor Christ and let him be the Lord of your life. Always be ready to give an answer when someone asks you about your hope. Give a kind and respectful answer and keep your conscience clear. This way you will make people ashamed for saying bad things about your good conduct as a follower of Christ. You are better off to obey God and suffer for doing right than to suffer for doing wrong" (1 Pet. 3:15–17, CEV).

CHAPTER 4

CURSED by SPIRITS of INFIRMITY

"An evil disease," they say, "clings to him. And now that he lies down, he will rise up no more."
—Psalm 41:8, NKJV

I

N BIBLE TIMES, fatal diseases were considered a thing of Belial. The Revised Standard Version says, "A deadly thing has fastened upon him; he will not rise again from where he lies."

Belial also has a host of spirits of infirmity and sickness that operate under him. Wherever there is immorality, there will be sickness and death. These are curses that come upon those who are perverse and crooked. Remember, Belial desires to draw men into sin, immorality, and perversion in order to bring the curse of the Lord upon a nation.

"Whoremongers and adulterers God will judge" (Heb. 13:4). It is possible that AIDS is a thing of Belial that cleaves to a person. AIDS is undoubtedly the result of sin, homosexuality, fornication, perversion, and drug abuse. AIDS is fatal, and in the natural, there is no cure. The New Living Translation of Psalm 41:8 says, "'He has some fatal disease,' they say. 'He will never get out of that bed!'"

The context of Psalm 41 is again the attacks of Belial against David, the Lord's anointed. David states, "All who hate me whisper together against me; against me they devise my hurt" (Ps. 41:7, NKJV). Again, Belial is mentioned in this context. I believe that as an End Time spirit, Belial has been released by the enemy to attack ministry gifts.

These can also include curses of *witchcraft* against true servants of the Lord, which often manifest through sickness. Leaders need strong prayer support against these spirits that are released under the strongman Belial, who hates and seeks to destroy ministry gifts.

PRAYERS

Lord, Your Word promises, "And ye shall serve the LORD your God, and he shall bless thy bread, and thy water; and I will take sickness away from the midst of thee" (Exod. 23:25).

Father, I want to serve You in honesty and obedience, for Your Word promises, "Because you listen to these judgments, and keep and do them...you shall be blessed above all peoples; there shall not be a male or female barren among you or among your livestock. And the LORD will take away from you all sickness, and will afflict you with none of the terrible diseases of Egypt which you have known" (Deut. 7:12, 14–15, NKJV).

Lord, when You walked on Earth, You "went about all Galilee, teaching in their synagogues, preaching the gospel of the kingdom, and healing all kinds of sickness and all kinds of disease among the people" (Matt. 4:23, NKJV). Walk today among my family and loved ones, Lord. Heal "all kinds of sickness and all kinds of disease" that try to afflict my loved ones, through Your holy power.

Father, give me faith as strong as the leper who "came and worshiped" You, saying, "Lord, if You are willing, You can make me clean." Your Word says that immediately You "put out [Your] hand and touched him, saying, 'I am willing; be cleansed'" (Matt. 8:2–3, NKJV). Immediately that leper's disease was cleansed because of his faith.

Jesus, You are the Great Physician. Your life on Earth was filled with miracles of healing. When a centurion asked You to heal his sick servant at home, You said, "I will go and heal him." But that man had enough faith in Your power to heal that he said, "But just say the word, and my servant will be healed." You honored his faith and told him, "Go! It will be done just as you believed it would" (Matt. 8:7–8, 13, NIV). And his servant was healed at that very hour.

Jesus, when You visited Peter's home, You discovered that his mother-in-law was "lying in bed with a fever." You "touched her hand and the fever left her, and she got up and began to wait on [You]" (Matt. 8:14–15, NKJV). What an awesome healer You are!

Lord, help me to be like those who believed so much in Your healing power that "they brought to Him many who were demon-possessed. And He cast out the spirits with a word, and healed all who were sick" (Matt. 8:16, NKJV). Truly You are the Great Physician who "took up our infirmities and carried our diseases" (v. 17, NIV).

Lord, in Your infinite wisdom You know that not only our bodies need Your healing touch, but our souls need Your healing too. When a paralyzed man was brought to You for physical healing, You first healed him spiritually by forgiving his sins. Then You told him, "'Get up, take your mat and go home.' And the man got up and went home" (Matt. 9:6–7, NIV).

Lord, when the Pharisees asked Your disciples why You would sit down and eat with tax collectors and sinners, You told them, "It is not the healthy who need a doctor, but the sick. But go and learn what this means: 'I desire mercy, not sacrifice.' For I have not come to call the righteous, but sinners" (Matt. 9:12–13, NIV). Help me to understand that in mercy, You have called me and healed me—physically and spiritually.

Lord, Your healing power is so powerful that it can raise the dead. When You went to a ruler's home and saw that his daughter had died and the crowd was already following their tradition of mourning the dead, You told them, "Go away. The girl is not dead but asleep." You ignored their laughing disbelief, made them go outside, and "went in and took the girl by the hand, and she got up" (Matt. 9:24–25, NIV). I will believe in Your power to heal and raise the dead, Lord, and will not doubt Your Word.

Jesus, when a woman who had suffered with a blood disease for twelve years reached out in faith to touch the edge of Your garment, You saw her and told her, "Take heart, daughter...your faith has healed you." And she was "healed from that moment" (Matt. 9: 22, NIV). Give me faith like her, Lord.

Lord, when two blind men followed You and asked You to heal them, You asked them, "Do you believe that I am able to do this?" They quickly responded, "Yes, Lord," and You touched their eyes and healed them. May I never forget the words You spoke to them: "According to your faith will it be done to you" (Matt. 9:27–30, NIV). Enlarge my faith, Lord, to believe in the impossible!

Lord, You "went through all the towns and villages, teaching in their synagogues, preaching the good news of the kingdom and healing every disease and sickness" (Matt. 9:35, NIV). You had compassion on people and described them as "harassed and helpless, like sheep without a shepherd" (v. 36). Just as then, Lord, "the harvest is plentiful but the workers are few" (v. 37). Send me out as a worker in Your harvest field. Help me to spread the news of Your power to heal and to save.

When You called Your twelve disciples, Lord, You "gave them power over unclean spirits, to cast them out, and to heal all kinds of sickness and all kinds of disease" (Matt. 10:1, NKJV). Help me to understand that You have called me to be Your disciple and that You have given me the same power to cast out demons—even the wicked spirit of Belial—and to heal sickness and disease.

Lord, You told Your disciples, "Go, preach, saying, 'The kingdom of heaven is at hand.' Heal the sick, cleanse the lepers, raise the dead, cast out demons. Freely you have received, freely give" (Matt. 10:7–8, NKJV). I am Your disciple, and I will follow Your command to GO.

Father, help me to understand that I am ministering to You when I serve others. When the disciples asked You, "Lord, when did we see You hungry and feed You, or thirsty and give You drink? When did we see You a stranger and take You in, or naked and clothe You? Or when did we see You sick, or in prison, and come to You?" Your response to them is the same response You give to me: "Assuredly, I say to you, inasmuch as you did it to one of the least of these My brethren, you did it to Me" (Matt. 25:37–40, NKJV).

Father, You gave a wonderful promise in Your Word for those who believe in You. You demonstrated that Your power was greater than the evil powers of Belial, for You promised to those who are saved, "Everyone who believes me will be able to do wonderful things. By using my name they will force out demons, and they will speak new languages. They will handle snakes and will drink poison and not be hurt. They will also heal sick people by placing their hands on them" (Mark 16:17–18, CEV).

Father, give me a spirit like Peter, who, after he was filled with Your Holy Spirit, was so full of Your power that "they brought the sick out into the streets and laid them on beds and couches, that at least the shadow of Peter passing by might fall on some of them" (Acts 5:14–16, NKJV).

Lord, give me the confidence that Peter had to know that he had been filled with Your power to heal. When he saw a man who had been bedridden for eight years with palsy, he told the man, "Jesus Christ has healed you! Get up and make up your bed." Right away he stood up (Acts 9:34, CEV).

Father, when a wonderful Greek Christian woman in Joppa who "was always doing good things for people and had given much to the poor...got sick and died," the followers sent for Peter to come to heal her. After he sent the mourners out of the room, he said to her, "Tabitha, get up!" When she opened her eyes and saw Peter, she sat up, and he took her by the hand and helped her to her feet (Acts 9:36–41, CEV). This story teaches me to be busy doing good things for others, because You will always take care of me.

Lord, You gave great healing power to Paul, as you did Peter. Your Word tells us, "God gave Paul the power to work great miracles. People even took handkerchiefs and aprons that had touched Paul's body, and they carried them to everyone who was sick. All of the sick people were healed, and the evil spirits went out" (Acts 19:11–12, CEV). Give me Your supernatural healing power too, and let me heal the sick and cast out the spirit of Belial at work in our world today.

Father, Your glorious healing power even protected Paul from the bite of a dangerous snake. He shook that snake off, just as we have the power to shake off the spirit of Belial. That was a mighty witness to everyone around, and it gave Paul the opportunity to heal anyone who was sick on the island (Acts 28:3–9). Let Your healing power at work in me be a mighty witness of Your power and glory.

Father, we are commanded in Your Word, "If you are sick, ask the church leaders to come and pray for you. Ask them to put olive oil on you in the name of the Lord. If you have faith when you pray for sick people, they will get well. The Lord will heal them, and if they have sinned, he will forgive them. If you have sinned, you should tell each other what you have done. Then you can pray for one another and be healed. The prayer of an innocent person is powerful, and it can help a lot" (James 5:14–16, CEV).

What a wonderful promise You have given to us, Lord. "Believing-prayer will heal you, and Jesus will put you on your feet. And if you've sinned, you'll be forgiven—healed inside and out" (James 5:15, THE MESSAGE).

CHAPTER 5

THE SPIRITS OF ALCOHOL AND DRUNKENNESS

Now Hannah spoke in her heart; only her lips moved, but her voice was not heard. Therefore Eli thought she was drunk. So Eli said to her, "How long will you be drunk? Put your wine away from you!" And Hannah answered and said, "No, my lord, I am a woman of sorrowful spirit. I have drunk neither wine nor intoxicating drink, but have poured out my soul before the LORD. Do not consider your maidservant a wicked woman, for out of the abundance of my complaint and grief I have spoken until now."
—1 Samuel 1:13–16, NKJV

IN THE KING James Version, verse 16 says, "Count not thine handmaid for a daughter of Belial." Eli had thought that Hannah was drunk. The spirit of Belial operates through *alcohol* and *drunkenness*. Drunkenness is a way to break down the morals and open people up to *lust* and *perversion*. I believe that spirits of alcohol and drunkenness operate under the strongman of Belial.

It is a known fact that many children of alcoholic parents are often the victims of sexual abuse, including incest. Alcohol can also open the door for *spirits of rape*, including "date rape" (which is so prevalent on many college campuses).

Proverbs warns us of the dangers of alcohol:

> Do not look on the wine when it is red,
> When it sparkles in the cup,
> When it swirls around smoothly;
> At the last it bites like a serpent,
> And stings like a viper.
> Your eyes will see strange things,
> And your heart will utter perverse things.
>
> —Proverbs 23:31–33, NKJV

These verses show the connection of the spirit of perversion to drunkenness. *To pervert* means "to cause to turn aside or away from what is good or true or morally right, to corrupt, to cause to turn aside from what is generally done or accepted."

Sexual perversion has become rampant in our nation with the promotion of homosexuality and lesbianism as acceptable and alternate lifestyles. These are *perversions* according to the Word of God. Spirits of perversion, including homosexuality and lesbianism, operate under the strongman of Belial. This is also referred to in the Word of God as *sodomy*.

Sodomy is defined as "copulation with a member of the same sex or with an animal (bestiality)." It is also noncoital, especially anal or oral copulation, with a member of the opposite sex. The term *sodomite* is mentioned five times in the Old Testament.

Sodomites were temple prostitutes who were a part of the worship of the idol gods of fertility in Canaan. These vile acts were a part of the idol worship of the Canaanites.

THE SONS OF ELI

> Now the sons of Eli were corrupt; they did not know the LORD.... Now Eli was very old; and he heard everything his sons did to all Israel, and how they lay with the women who assembled at the door of the tabernacle of meeting.
>
> —1 Samuel 2:12, 22, NKJV

The sons of Eli represent *ministry*. They, along with Eli, were in charge of the priesthood, regulating the temple, and the sacrifices of Israel. Their abuses brought the judgment of the Lord upon them and the establishment of a new order under Samuel. These sons are called "sons of Belial." They were being motivated and controlled by the spirit of Belial.

One of the works of Belial is to bring uncleanness into the temple of God. The ministry is a target of this spirit. He

45

desires to draw the servant of the Lord, His anointed, into sin (especially sexual sin) to bring reproach to the church.

These priests were also guilty of greed in making themselves "fat with the best of all the offerings of Israel" (1 Sam. 2:29, NKJV). Their sin was so great that "men abhorred the offering of the LORD" (v. 17).

> If one man sins against another, God will judge him. But if a man sins against the LORD, who will intercede for him?" Nevertheless they did not heed the voice of their father, because the LORD desired to kill them.
>
> —1 Samuel 2:25, NKJV

The Rotherham translation says, "...for Yahweh was pleased to put them to death." The Lord judged their sin with death. There is no reason for this kind of activity, especially from those who are in the ministry. God forbids men of God to lie with the women of their congregations.

The spirit of Belial desires to draw the servants of God into this kind of hideous activity in order to bring curses and judgment upon the servants of the Lord. The sons of Eli "knew not the LORD" (1 Sam. 2:12). True apostles, prophets, evangelists, pastors, and teachers know the Lord. They also know that there are moral standards by which God's servants are expected to live.

Remember, "whoremongers and adulterers God will judge" (Heb. 13:4). God told Eli:

> For I have told him that I will judge his house forever
> for the iniquity which he knows, because his sons
> made themselves vile, and he did not restrain them.
> —1 Samuel 3:13, NKJV

This verse tells us the Lord considered their acts *vile*. The Berkeley translation says, "His sons were bringing a curse upon themselves." The Revised Standard Version says, "...because his sons were blaspheming God."

Again, the work of Belial is to cause men to get involved in sins that are abominable and bring the curse of God.

> ...who, knowing the righteous judgment of God,
> that those who practice such things are worthy of
> death, not only do the same but also approve of
> those who practice them.
>
> —Romans 1:32, NKJV

What sins does Paul mention that are worthy of death? The answer is *idolatry*, *homosexuality*, and *lesbianism*. Now, I am not stating that every person involved in these sins should be put to death. Thank God for His mercy. There is salvation offered to all. Jesus died and shed His blood for sin. Those who repent and accept His sacrifice will receive deliverance and forgiveness of sin.

However, the judgment of God does come to those who, through a hard and impenitent heart, will not repent (Rom. 2:5). Regardless of what the secular media try to

47

tell us concerning homosexuality and lesbianism, these are perversions and are under the judgment of God.

> For this reason God gave them up to vile passions. For even their women exchanged the natural use for what is against nature. Likewise also the men, leaving the natural use of the woman, burned in their lust for one another, men with men committing what is shameful, and receiving in themselves the penalty of their error which was due.
>
> —Romans 1:26–27, NKJV

The Phillips translation calls them "disgraceful passions." The Knox version says "disgraceful acts." The Conybeare translation says, "…men with men working abomination."

Webster's definition of *abomination* is "extreme disgust and hatred, loathing." *Loathe* means "to dislike greatly and often with disgust or intolerance, to detest."

> And even as they did not like to retain God in their knowledge, God gave them over to a debased mind, to do those things which are not fitting.
>
> —Romans 1:28, NKJV

Reprobate spirits also operate with homosexuality and perversion. The dictionary definition of *reprobate* is "rejected as worthless, morally abandoned, depraved." You will recall that the definition of *Belial* is "worthlessness."

When something is reprobate, it has been judged by God as worthless and, therefore, rejected. The Revised Standard

Version says, "God gave them up to a base mind." The word *base* means "to be of little value." Synonyms include *low* and *vile*, meaning, "deserving contempt because of the absence of higher values, disgusting depravity or filth."

Belial is a wicked ruler that leads men into sins that are base and vile. Reprobate spirits and spirits of homosexuality and lesbianism operate under Belial, cursing men to commit vile acts, thus bringing the judgment of God.

The apostle Paul goes on to mention a host of evil spirits that come in once the mind becomes reprobate:

> Being filled with all unrighteousness, sexual immorality, wickedness, covetousness, maliciousness; full of envy, murder, strife, deceit, evil-mindedness; they are whisperers, backbiters, haters of God, violent, proud, boasters, inventors of evil things, disobedient to parents, undiscerning, untrustworthy, unloving, unforgiving, unmerciful.
>
> —Romans 1:29–31, NKJV

These verses say that they are *filled* with these things. This is obviously a list of demons that enter and dwell in those who are guilty of *base sins*. In other words, those guilty of these sins had become demonized.

Unclean sexual acts attract curses from unclean spirits. The only solution is repentance and deliverance.

PRAYERS

DRUNKENNESS

Father, help me to listen to the warning in Your Word to "take heed to yourselves, lest your hearts be weighed down with carousing, drunkenness, and cares of this life." Keep me focused on living for You, so that I am not caught in the devil's snare to cause me to be unprepared when "that Day come on you unexpectedly" (Luke 21:34, NKJV).

Father, help me to "live and conduct [myself] honorably and becomingly as in the [open light of] day, not in reveling (carousing) and drunkenness, not in immorality and debauchery (sensuality and licentiousness), not in quarreling and jealousy" (Rom. 13:13, AMP).

Lord, I want to do only what You want me to do, for following my own desires will lead me astray. "People's desires make them give in to immoral ways, filthy thoughts, and shameful deeds. They worship idols, practice witchcraft, hate others, and are hard to get along with. People become jealous, angry, and selfish. They not only argue and cause trouble, but they are envious. They get drunk, carry on at wild parties, and do other evil things as well"

(Gal. 5:19–21, CEV). I don't want to live like that, Lord. I want to honor and serve You in everything I do.

Father, You give good advice in Your Word—advice I want to follow: "Oh listen, dear child—become wise; point your life in the right direction. Don't drink too much wine and get drunk; don't eat too much food and get fat. Drunks and gluttons will end up on skid row, in a stupor and dressed in rags" (Prov. 23:21, THE MESSAGE).

Father, Your Word warns me to be careful about the kind of people I hang around with. Help me to heed Your advice to "not associate with anyone who calls himself a brother but is sexually immoral or greedy, an idolater or a slanderer, a drunkard or a swindler" (1 Cor. 5:11, NIV). Help me to choose my friends wisely.

Lord, I do not want to "be drunk with wine, in which is dissipation." I want to be "filled with the Spirit" (Eph. 5:18, NKJV). Fill me with Your Spirit, Lord.

God, from the time of Aaron, You have instructed Your Christian leaders and ministers: "When you enter the Tent of Meeting, don't drink wine or strong drink, neither you nor your sons, lest you die.

This is a fixed rule down through the generations. Distinguish between the holy and the common" (Lev. 10:8–10, The Message). May I never fail You by making what is holy common by my sinfulness and drunkenness.

Father, You taught that anyone who is "consecrating yourself totally to God" should not "drink any wine or beer, no intoxicating drink of any kind" (Num. 6:2, The Message). Help me to understand that drunkenness destroys my ability to stay consecrated to You, and help me to turn away from that which has the power to turn me away from You.

Lord, help me to follow the simple advice of Your Word, which says, "It isn't smart to get drunk! Drinking makes a fool of you and leads to fights" (Prov. 20:1, cev).

Father, You have strong advice about the dangers of drunkenness for those who are called to be leaders, for in Your Word, You say, "Kings and leaders should not get drunk or even want to drink" (Prov. 31:4, cev). Help me to honor Your Word in this matter.

Lord, help me to understand how easily Satan can trap us in the bondage of alcoholism. It becomes so powerful that it takes over a person's life. Your

Word reminds us of this by saying, "You are in for trouble! You get up early to start drinking, and you keep it up late into the night. At your drinking parties you have the music of stringed instruments, tambourines, and flutes. But you never even think about all the Lord has done, and so his people know nothing about him" (Isa. 5:11–13, CEV).

Father, the enemy blinds us to the dangers of drunkenness and alcoholism, and Your Word describes how it affects our actions: "You think you are clever and smart. And you are great at drinking and mixing drinks. But you are in for trouble. You accept bribes to let the guilty go free, and you cheat the innocent out of a fair trial. You will go up in flames like straw and hay! You have rejected the teaching of the holy Lord God All-Powerful of Israel. Now your roots will rot, and your blossoms will turn to dust" (Isa. 5:21–24, CEV).

Father, wake up the spiritual leaders of the world today to understand Your disgust at their drunkenness. Your Word says, "Priests and prophets stumble because they are drunk. Their minds are too confused to receive God's messages or give honest decisions.... You drunken leaders are like babies! How can you possibly understand or teach the Lord's message? You don't even listen—all you hear is senseless sound after senseless sound" (Isa. 28:7, 9–10, CEV).

PERVERSENESS

Father, Your Word tells me You are "the Rock; [Your] deeds are perfect. Everything [You do] is just and fair. [You are] a faithful God who does no wrong; how just and upright [You are]!" But there are many people who have "acted corruptly toward [You]; when they act so perversely, are they really [Your] children? They are a deceitful and twisted generation" (Deut. 32:4–5, NLT). Father, may everything I do show others that You are my Rock. Cleanse me from all perverseness.

Father, I know that sometimes I will fail You and sin against You. Help me to remember what Your Word says to do when that happens: "When [I] sin against you—for there is no one who does not sin—and you become angry with [me] and give [me] over to the enemy...if [I] have a change of heart...and say, '[I] have sinned, [I] have done wrong, [I] have acted wickedly'; and if [I] turn back to you with all [my] heart and soul...and pray to you...then from heaven, your dwelling place," You will "hear [my] prayer and...forgive all the offenses [I] have committed against you" (1 Kings 8:46–50, NIV).

Thank You for forgiving me and showing mercy to me, Lord.

Father, help me to "put away perversity from [my] mouth" and to "keep corrupt talk far from [my] lips" (Prov. 4:24, NIV).

Lord, teach me to seek after integrity, for Your Word tells us, "The integrity of the upright shall guide them, but the willful contrariness and crookedness of the treacherous shall destroy them" (Prov. 11:3, AMP).

Father, protect me from drunkenness and alcoholism and from perversity of any kind. May I be so completely consecrated to Your will for my life that I willingly "do everything without complaining or arguing, so that [I] may become blameless and pure," a child of God "without fault in a crooked and depraved generation," so that I may shine with the light of Your love as I serve You and "hold out the word of life" to those around me (Phil. 2:14–16, NIV).

CHAPTER 6

SPIRITS BRINGING CURSES OF RAPE and SEXUAL ABUSE

Now as they were making their hearts merry, behold, the men of the city, certain sons of Belial, beset the house round about, and beat at the door, and spake to the master of the house, the old man, saying, Bring forth the man that came into thine house, that we may know him. And the man, the master of the house, went out unto them, Nay, my brethren, nay, I pray you, do not so wickedly; seeing that this man is come into mine house, do not this folly. Behold, here is my daughter a maiden, and his concubine; them I will bring out now, and humble ye them, and do with them what seemeth good unto you: but unto this man do not so vile a thing. But the men would not hearken to him: so the man took his concubine, and brought her forth unto them; and they knew her, and abused her all the night until the morning: and when the day began to spring, they let her go.
—Judges 19:22–25

THE NEW INTERNATIONAL Version says, "They raped her and abused her throughout the night." This is one of the *vilest* acts recorded in the Word of God. The "sons of Belial" raped the concubine until the next morning. As we continue reading through to the end of the chapter, we find that the concubine actually *died* from this vile act committed against her. She was literally *raped to death*.

> At daybreak the woman went back to the house where her master was staying, fell down at the door and lay there until daylight. When her master got up in the morning and opened the door of the house and stepped out to continue on his way, there lay his concubine, fallen in the doorway of the house, with her hands on the threshold. He said to her, "Get up; let's go." But there was no answer. Then the man put her on his donkey and set out for home.
>
> —Judges 19:26–28, NIV

The Amplified Version says, "But there was no answer [for she was dead]." What happens next is very graphic:

> When he reached home, he took a knife and cut up his concubine, limb by limb, into twelve parts and sent them into all the areas of Israel. Everyone who saw it said, "Such a thing has never been seen or done, not since the day the Israelites came up out of Egypt."
>
> —Judges 19:29–30, NIV

The Amplified Version says, "There was no such deed done or seen from the day that the Israelites came up out of the land of Egypt to this day." The Contemporary English Version says, "This is horrible! Nothing like this has ever happened since the day Israel left Egypt." The New Living Translation says, "Such a horrible crime has not been committed in all the time since Israel left Egypt."

This abominable act caused civil war in Israel.

> So I took hold of my concubine, cut her in pieces, and sent her throughout all the territory of the inheritance of Israel, because they committed lewdness and outrage in Israel.
>
> —Judges 20:6, NKJV

The Word of God calls this act "lewdness." *Webster's* defines *lewd* as "evil, wicked, sexually unchaste or licentious, obscene, salacious." The word *obscene* means "disgusting to the senses, repulsive." Thus, Belial causes men to commit vile and obscene acts.

Other spirits working under Belial include rape and sexual abuse. The concubine was raped and abused until she died as a result. The proliferation of rape and sexual abuse, including *incest* and *sodomy*, is the result of the wicked spirit of Belial.

I have ministered to thousands of women and men who were the victims of sexual abuse as children. I also have cast out *spirits of death* that came in during the violation.

When someone is violated in this way, it can be like a death entering that person's soul.

Today, the curse of sexual abuse is rampant in our nation. These filthy spirits are the work of the wicked ruler Belial.

> So all the men of Israel were gathered against the city, united together as one man. Then the tribes of Israel sent men through all the tribe of Benjamin, saying, "What is this wickedness that has occurred among you? Now therefore, deliver up the men, the perverted men who are in Gibeah, that we may put them to death and remove the evil from Israel!" But the children of Benjamin would not listen to the voice of their brethren, the children of Israel.
>
> —Judges 20:11–13, NKJV

The tribes of Israel were so repulsed by this act of mass rape that they gathered together against the city of Gibeah and demanded those who were guilty of this act. They decided to put to death the guilty.

There is much controversy today in America concerning the *death penalty*. Many liberals in our nation think it is a cruel method that needs to be outlawed. However, in the Word of God, there were sins that were abominable enough to merit the death penalty. This book is not debating the pros and cons of the death penalty, but suffice it to say that it is found in the Word of God.

The *spirit of Belial* desires for us to tolerate these vile acts in our nation. But there are some sins that are so vile and abominable that they will stir moral indignation in most people, saved or unsaved. The abominable spirits that operate under Belial inflicting curses upon people include spirits of rape, incest, molestation, sexual abuse, sexual impurity, uncleanness, filthiness, lasciviousness, sodomy, lewdness, and obscenity.

PRAYERS

ABOMINATIONS

Father, Your Word instructs, "You shall not lie with a male as with a woman. It is an abomination" (Lev. 18:22, NKJV). Reveal the abominable sin of homosexuality in America, Lord, and bring Your people to repentance.

Lord, Your Word reveals a listing of the abominable sexual perversions that You will judge. Many of these things can be seen in our nation today. They include "anyone who is near of kin to him, to uncover his nakedness." You include the following relatives in this warning: father, mother, father's wife, sister, the daughter of my father, the daughter of my mother, son's daughter, daughter's daughter, father's wife's daughter, father's sister, mother's sister, father's brother, his wife, daughter-in-law, brother's wife, a woman and her daughter, her son's daughter, and her daughter's daughter (Lev. 18:6–19, NKJV).

Lord, it is Your instruction that a man is not to engage in sexual relations with his neighbor's wife, or a woman with her neighbor's husband (Lev. 18:20, NKJV).

Father, You give clear instructions that no person is to offer his or her own children as a sacrifice to a false idol or as a sacrifice during a false idolatrous ritual (Lev. 18:21, NKJV). Father, forgive America for sacrificing millions of unborn children annually on the altar of abortion.

God, it is an abomination to You for a man or woman to mate with any animal. Your Word calls this "perversion" (Lev. 18:23, NKJV).

Father, You have said that the nation that allows these abominable things to take place is defiled and have promised to cast it away. You will visit iniquity upon it until the land vomits out its inhabitants (Lev. 18:27–28, NKJV).

God, Your Word declares, "Whoever commits any of these abominations, the persons who commit them shall be cut off from among their people" (Lev. 18:29,

NKJV). God, call America to repentance for its sexual depravity and sin. Redeem Your people and save us.

Lord, these six things You hate; yes, seven are an abomination to You (Prov. 6:16–20, NKJV):

- A proud look
- A lying tongue
- Hands that shed innocent blood
- A heart that devises wicked plans
- Feet that are swift in running to evil
- A false witness who speaks lies
- One who sows discord among brethren

CROSS-DRESSING

Father, Your Word declares: "Women must not pretend to be men [or wear men's clothing], and men must not pretend to be women [or wear women's clothing]. The LORD your God is disgusted with people who do that" (Deut. 22:5, CEV).

PROSTITUTION

Father, You are "disgusted with men and women who are prostitutes of any kind, and [You] will not accept a gift from them, even if it had been promised" (Deut. 23:18, CEV).

SEXUAL IMPURITY IN THE CHURCH

Father, just as You warned the children of Israel that You would reject and abandon them for allowing sexual impurity and idolatry to take place in the temple, so You are warning America's churches of the evil within. You declare, "The people of Judah have done evil in my eyes, declares the LORD. They have set up their detestable idols in the house that bears my Name and have defiled it" (Jer. 7:30, NIV).

Father, just as in the Bible, the sexual impurity in the churches of America has been exposed and revealed throughout the land. God is saying to America, as He said to Israel, "This is your lot, the portion measured to you from Me, says the Lord, because you have forgotten Me and trusted in falsehood [false gods and alliances with idolatrous nations]. Therefore I Myself will [retaliate], throwing your skirts up over your face, that your shame [of being clad like a slave] may be exposed. I have seen your detestable acts, even your adulteries and your lustful neighings [after idols], and the lewdness of your harlotry on the hills in the field. Woe to you, O Jerusalem! For how long a time yet will you not [meet My conditions and] be made clean?" (Jer. 13:25–27, AMP). Father, call America to repentance, and forgive our land for the rampant sexual immorality, even in Your church.

Father, cause Your people to take heed to Your warning, which states, "But when good people start sinning and doing disgusting things, will they live? No! All their good deeds will be forgotten, and they will be put to death because of their sins" (Ezek. 18:24, cev). May we recognize the danger of allowing impurity to creep into Your church, and may we turn from our wicked ways.

God, You gave Your prophet Ezekiel a hard message, and the truth of Your words must be understood by Your people today, for America has sinned as Israel did. Your warning is strong and fearsome: "God the Master says…you worship no-god idols, you murder at will—and you expect to own this land? You rely on the sword, you engage in obscenities, you indulge in sex at random—anyone, anytime. And you still expect to own this land?…As sure as I am the living God…I'll make this country an empty wasteland….They'll realize that I am God when I devastate the country because of all the obscenities they've practiced" (Ezek. 33:25–29, The Message). Father, hear our plea and spare our land!

Father, may we avoid the horrible results of sin that are demonstrated to us through the example of the Romans. Your Word tells us, "Because they exchanged the truth of God for a lie and worshiped and served the creature rather than the Creator…God gave them over and abandoned them to vile affections and degrading passions. For their women exchanged their natural function for an unnatural and abnormal one, and the men also turned from natural relations with women and were set ablaze (burning out, consumed) with lust for one another—men committing shameful acts with men and suffering in their own bodies and personalities the inevitable consequences and penalty of their wrong-doing and going astray, which was [their] fitting retribution. And so, since they did not see fit to acknowledge God or approve of Him or consider Him worth the knowing, God gave them over to a base and condemned mind to do things not proper or decent but loathsome, until they were filled (permeated and saturated) with every kind of unrighteousness" (Rom. 2:25–29, AMP).

Father, cause the people of America to hear Your clear instructions to "kill (deaden, deprive of power) the evil desire lurking in your members [those animal impulses and all that is earthly in you that is employed in sin]: sexual vice, impurity, sensual appetites, unholy desires, and all greed and covetousness, for that is idolatry" (Col. 3:5, AMP). Save our nation, God, and call us to repentance.

Lord, You give us clear advice: "Therefore, get rid of all moral filth and the evil that is so prevalent and humbly accept the word planted in you, which can save you" (James 1:21, NIV). Turn us from our sexual impurity and lust, and let Your Word be firmly planted within our hearts and lives, that we may be saved.

CHAPTER 7

CURSED by PORNOGRAPHY and PEDOPHILIA

I will set nothing wicked before my eyes; I hate the work of those who fall away; it shall not cling to me.
—Psalm 101:3, NKJV

THE NEW AMERICAN Standard Bible says, "I will set no worthless thing before my eyes." This shows us the attitude and abhorrence we, as people of God, should have toward anything related to Belial. We should resist and abhor anything base, vile, unworthy, unclean, ungodly, contemptible, wicked, blasphemous, or shameful.

We are to abhor that which is evil and cleave to that which is good. *Abhor* is a strong word. It means "to regard with extreme repugnance, to loathe; to turn aside or keep away from, especially in scorn or shuddering fear, to reject, to hate."

This verse can apply to the present-day rise of pornography and the sexual filth that Belial is flooding our nation with. One of the vilest forms of pornography is "kiddie porn," which is a thriving business supported by pedophiles. *Pedophilia* is sexual perversion in which children are the preferred sexual objects.

Most states have obscenity laws that are being challenged by those who feel as if government should provide no constraint. *Obscenity* is defined as "the state of being obscene." *Obscene* means "disgusting to the senses, repulsive, abhorrent to morality or virtue."

Pornography opens the door for a host of evil spirits of lust and perversion. There has also been a connection between pornography and rape in some studies. I believe Belial is a ruling spirit over spirits of pornography, whoredom, prostitution, and other sexual spirits.

Sexual impurity is another strong spirit that is under Belial's control, including spirits of homosexuality and lesbianism (perversion). If this spirit can pervert the morals of a nation through sexual immorality, he can bring the judgment and curse of the Lord upon a nation.

PRAYERS

Lord, Your Word describes the actions of a child molester as "a wicked man" who "hunts down the weak, who are caught in the schemes he devises." You describe this wicked person who "lies in wait near the villages…watching in secret for his victims. He lies in wait like a lion in cover; he lies in wait to catch the helpless; he catches the helpless and drags them off in his net. His victims are crushed, they collapse; they fall under his strength" (Ps. 10:2, 8–10, NIV). Protect the children of this nation from such wickedness, Lord, and bring Your judgment down upon these wicked predators.

Father, our nation is filled with the impurities and perverseness of men and women who do only what is "right in [their] own eyes" (Judg. 17:6, NKJV). Reveal Your righteousness to America, Lord, and cause us to "lift up [our] eyes to the hills," for our "help comes from the LORD, the Maker of heaven and earth" (Ps. 121:1–3, NIV).

Father, Your Word tells us that wickedness begins in our eyes. It is when we take our eyes off You and place them on worldly things that we are enticed and drawn away by our sinful lust (James 1:14, NKJV).

THE PROGRESSION OF PORNOGRAPHY

Father, pornography is an insidious evil that begins with a first glance at someone immodestly dressed, and "we are tempted by our own desires that drag us off and trap us. Our desires make us sin, and when sin is finished with us, it leaves us dead" (James 1:14–15, CEV).

Lord, when we yield to the temptation to our eyes, those sinful activities become an addiction to us, and we become "a slave of sin" (John 8:34). When pornography has trapped a person, that person becomes a "slave of depravity—for a man is a slave to whatever has mastered him" (2 Pet. 2:19, NIV).

Lord, cause Americans who are addicted to the sinful allure of pornography to understand that Your Word teaches, "Can you build a fire in your lap and not burn your pants? Can you walk barefoot on hot coals and not get blisters?" (Prov. 6:27–28, THE MESSAGE). Reveal the burns of pornography upon the souls of Americans, and turn us away from its wicked entrapments.

Father, remove the stain of pornography from Your church. Help us to hear the cry of Peter, who warns, "I implore you as aliens and strangers and exiles [in this world] to abstain from the sensual urges (the evil desires, the passions of the flesh, your lower nature) that wage war against the soul" (1 Pet. 2:11, AMP).

Lord, keep us from believing that a little bit of sin— a little bit of pornography—won't hurt us. If we do not turn away from this sin, You will tell us plainly, "I never knew you. Away from me, you evildoers!" (Matt. 7:23, NIV).

Father, all the evils of sexual impurity—including pornography—make us "unclean" in Your sight. "For from within, out of men's hearts, come evil thoughts, sexual immorality, theft, murder, adultery, greed, malice, deceit, lewdness, envy, slander, arrogance and folly. All these evils come from inside and make a man 'unclean'" (Mark 7:20–23, NIV).

Lord, the sins of sexual impurity will separate us from You and cause You to hide Your face from us and refuse to hear us when we call (Isa. 59:2, NKJV).

Father, ultimately, if we continue to cling to pornographic images and thoughts, we will even be denied entrance into heaven. "Those who practice such things will not inherit the kingdom of God" (Gal. 5:21, NKJV).

God, because pornography can become an addiction that is hard to get free of, we must actively seek after Your Word and You to break its hold upon us. You tell us to, "Be on your guard and stay awake. Your enemy, the devil, is like a roaring lion, sneaking around to find someone to attack" (1 Pet. 5:8, CEV).

Father, You tell us in Your Word that we can keep our lives pure "by living according to your word." Help us to make this commitment: "I seek you with all my heart; do not let me stray from your commands. I have hidden your word in my heart that I might not sin against you" (Ps. 119:9–11, NIV).

Lord, there is one guaranteed way for me to live free of sexual impurity and the temptation of pornographic sin. Paul told us how to avoid sin when he said, "All I want is to know Christ and the power that raised him to life. . . . I have not yet reached my goal, and I am not perfect. But Christ has taken hold of me. . . . I don't feel that I have already arrived. But I forget what is behind, and I struggle for what is ahead. I run toward the goal, so that I can win the prize of being called to heaven. This is the prize that God offers because of what Christ Jesus has done. All of us who are mature should think in this same way. . . . We must keep going in the direction that we are now headed" (Phil. 3:10–16, CEV).

Father, how I thank You for this promise: "For no temptation (no trial regarded as enticing to sin), [no matter how it comes or where it leads] has overtaken you and laid hold on you that is not common to man [that is, no temptation or trial has come to you that is beyond human resistance and that is not adjusted and adapted and belonging to human experience, and such as man can bear]. But God is faithful [to His Word and to His compassionate nature], and He [can be trusted] not to let you be tempted and tried and assayed beyond your ability and strength of resistance and power to endure, but with the temptation He will [always] also provide the way out (the means of escape to a landing place), that you may be capable and strong and powerful to bear up under it patiently" (1 Cor. 10:13, AMP).

Lord, one of the greatest promises in Your Word is this: "My power is strongest when you are weak" (2 Cor. 12:9, CEV). With Your power, we can live free of the snare of pornography.

CHILD MOLESTATION AND PEDOPHILIA

Father, Your Word tells the horrible story of Amnon's brutal rape of his half sister, Tamar (2 Sam. 13:1–22). By that terrible sin, he became a pedophile, and he destroyed the life of Tamar and created hatred and animosity in King David's family that caused rejection, murder, and devastation. Father, wake America up to the devastation that this abhorrent sin of pedophilia and child molestation has caused. Call us to repentance, and bring down Your judgment on those who will not turn from their wicked ways.

Father, You said that if anyone hurts one of Your little children, "it would be better for him if a millstone were hung around his neck, and he were drowned in the depth of the sea" (Matt. 18:6, NKJV). Millions of Your little children have been devastated by the sin of molestation. We cry out to You for mercy and restoration for each one of them, and we pledge our lives to doing all we can to purge America of its pedophiles.

Father, in the strongest possible words, You warn us of the dangers of sin by saying, "If your hand or foot causes you to sin, cut it off and cast it from you. It is better for you to enter into life lame or maimed, rather than having two hands or two feet, to be cast into the everlasting fire. And if your eye causes you to sin, pluck it out and cast it from you. It is better for you to enter into life with one eye, rather than having two eyes, to be cast into hell fire" (Matt. 18:8–9, NKJV). You gave this warning in the context of warning those who hurt little children. Help us to understand the depth of Your love for children and to do everything we can to protect them in America.

CHILDREN ARE GOD'S BEST GIFTS

Teach us to value children the way You do, Lord. You have said, "Don't you see that children are GOD's best gift? The fruit of the womb his generous legacy? Like a warrior's fistful of arrows are the children of a vigorous youth. Oh, how blessed are you parents, with your quivers full of children! Your enemies don't stand a chance against you; you'll sweep them right off your doorstep" (Ps. 127:3–5, THE MESSAGE).

Father, You demonstrated Your love for children when the people crowded around You with their babies in the hope that You would bless them. When the disciples saw this, they tried to shoo off the parents. But You called them back and said, "Let these children alone. Don't get between them and me. These children are the kingdom's pride and joy. Mark this: Unless you accept God's kingdom in the simplicity of a child, you'll never get in" (Luke 18:16–17, THE MESSAGE). Teach me to live for You in the simplicity of childhood and to protect Your children from harm.

CHAPTER 8

CURSED WITH LAWLESSNESS
and REBELLION

*From you comes forth one who plots evil
against the LORD, a wicked counselor.*
—Nahum 1:11, NKJV

THE NEW JERUSALEM Bible says, "From you has emerged someone plotting evil against Yahweh, one of Belial's counsellors." Nahum is prophesying judgment against Nineveh and the Assyrian Empire. The king of Assyria was actually plotting against the Lord. One translation says, "Who is this king of yours who dares to plot against the Lord?"

This is the spirit of *antichrist.* Psalm 2:2–3 says, "The kings of the earth set themselves, and the rulers take counsel together, against the LORD and against His Anointed, saying, 'Let us break Their bonds in pieces and cast away Their cords from us'" (NKJV).

There you have it; the ultimate goal of Belial is to *cast*

76

off restraint. The church is a restraining force in the earth against the filth and ungodliness Belial desires to flood upon the earth.

The Amplified Bible says, "…and cast Their cords [of control] from us." These "kings of the earth" are the spirits of *lawlessness* and *rebellion*. While there is no law, people run wild.

America's entire judicial system was founded on the Judeo-Christian ethic found in the Bible. In other words, the Bible is the foundation of our legal system. A society that rejects the Bible as its moral authority will eventually have problems with its judicial system. Belial hates the restraining power of the Bible, the Holy Spirit, and the church. This is why he attacks them so viciously.

Belial desires immorality and ungodliness to reign without any restraint. Belial is responsible for an attack upon our judicial system that we are experiencing today in America. Laws against homosexuality, lesbianism, and adultery, which were once a part of our legal code, are now being removed.

Homosexuals believe they have a right to live ungodly lifestyles. Many are clamoring, "Leave me alone, and let me do what I want. I don't want any preacher to tell me what is right and wrong." Others are asserting, "Give us separation of church and state. Take prayer out of the schools." This is all an attempt to cast off restraint.

PRAYERS

RESTRAINT

Father, the faithful and godly minority in America has begun to feel as Job felt when he was being persecuted and mocked. His words describe our feelings, for he cried out, "Sons of the worthless and nameless...I am a byword to them. They abhor me, they stand aloof from me, and do not refrain from spitting in my face or at the sight of me...they have cast off the bridle [of restraint] before me. On my right hand rises the rabble brood; they jostle me and push away my feet, and they cast up against me their ways of destruction [like an advancing army]" (Job 30:8–12, AMP). Father, rescue us as You did Job, and restore restraint and godliness to America.

Lord, Your Word has clearly identified the reason America is falling into godlessness and immorality. You tell us clearly, "Where there is no revelation ['no vision (no redemptive revelation of God),' AMP], the people cast off restraint" (Prov. 29:18, NKJV). This nation has forsaken the restraints of Your Word for their own godless, liberal agendas. Have mercy on America, Lord, and reestablish us in Your laws.

Father, Your Word tells us what happened when Your people in Israel abandoned Your ways: "God indicts the whole population: 'No one is faithful. No one loves. No one knows the first thing about God. All this cussing and lying and killing, theft and loose sex, sheer anarchy, one murder after another! And because of all this, the very land itself weeps and everything in it is grief-stricken" (Hosea 4:1–3, THE MESSAGE). And You told the priests and prophets: "But don't look for someone to blame. No finger pointing!... Because you've turned your back on knowledge, I've turned my back on you priests. Because you refuse to recognize the revelation of God, I'm no longer recognizing your children" (vv. 4–10). This sounds like America today, Father. Forgive Your Christian leaders for turning our backs on Your revelation; redeem Your church, so we can lead America into righteousness.

REBELLION

Father, Your Word reveals Moses's disappointment with the Levites—Israel's spiritual leaders. When he was about to die, he called the Levites together, and he told them, "This is The Book of God's Law. Keep it beside the sacred chest that holds the agreement the LORD your God made with Israel. This book is proof that you know what the LORD wants you to do. I know how stubborn and rebellious you and the rest of the Israelites are. You have rebelled against the LORD while I have been alive, and it will only get worse after I am gone. So call together the leaders and officials of the tribes of Israel. I will bring this book and read every word of it to you, and I will call the sky and the earth as witnesses that all of you know what you are supposed to do. I am going to die soon, and I know that in the future you will stop caring about what is right and what is wrong, and so you will disobey the LORD and stop living the way I told you to live. The LORD will be angry, and terrible things will happen to you" (Deut. 31:26–29, CEV). His words describe a great host of America's spiritual leaders, Lord. Help me to continue to serve You with a godly and righteous heart, and keep me from failing You as others have.

Father, when Saul became so proud and arrogant that he disobeyed You, You sent Samuel to tell him, "Does the LORD really want sacrifices and offerings? No! He doesn't want your sacrifices. He wants you to obey him. Rebelling against God or disobeying him because you are proud is just as bad as worshiping idols or asking them for advice. You refused to do what God told you, so God has decided that you can't be king" (1 Sam. 15:22–23, CEV). Keep me from becoming rebellious, proud, and disobedient to You, Father. May You never have to say about me,

"I'm sorry that I gave you your ministry, because in your pride you failed to obey Me."

Father, after the children of Israel had wandered in the wilderness for forty years, You confronted them about their rebelliousness, and You told them, "Understand that the LORD your God is not giving you this good land to possess because of your righteousness, for you are a stiff-necked people. Remember! Do not forget how you provoked the LORD your God to wrath in the wilderness. From the day that you departed from the land of Egypt until you came to this place, you have been rebellious against the LORD" (Deut. 9:6–7, NKJV). Just as Moses pleaded with You to have mercy on the people and not destroy them, so I plead with You, Father, to forgive America for its rebelliousness and sin. I ask You to save our nation from destruction.

Lord, You place a high priority upon obedience. You are a "Father of orphans" and a "champion of widows." You make "homes for the homeless" and lead "prisoners to freedom." But You "leave rebels to rot in hell" (Ps. 68:6, THE MESSAGE).

Father, over and over in Your Word You extended mercy and grace to the rebellious Israelites. When they turned back to You, You forgave them and restored them to Your favor. You told them, "In returning and rest you shall be saved; in quietness and confidence shall be your strength" (Isa. 30:15, NKJV). You waited for them to return to You so that You could show them Your grace and mercy, for You are a God of justice (v. 18). Father, we plead for You to be patient and wait for America to turn back to You. Show us Your grace and mercy, Father, that we may return in obedience to serving You.

EVIL IMAGINATIONS

Lord, Paul gave a warning about those who turn away from You: "Yes, they knew God, but they wouldn't worship him as God or even give him thanks. And they began to think up foolish ideas of what God was like. As a result, their minds became dark and confused. Claiming to be wise, they instead became utter fools" (Rom. 1:21–22, NLT). So many people in our world today have made up foolish ideas about You, and as a result have minds that have become dark and confused. They profess to be part of a "new age," but they look like fools. Lord, raise up a godly army that will keep these fools from confusing and pulling others away from You. Move by Your Holy Spirit to destroy the influence of those who claim to know more than You.

Lord, make us into a strong, bold spiritual army in America. "We are human, but we don't wage war as humans do. We use God's mighty weapons, not worldly weapons, to knock down the strongholds of human reasoning and to destroy false arguments. We destroy every proud obstacle that keeps people from knowing God. We capture their rebellious thoughts and teach them to obey Christ" (2 Cor. 10:3–5, NLT).

EVIL

Lord, "You are not a God who takes pleasure in evil," and "the wicked cannot dwell" with You. "The arrogant cannot stand in your presence," and "you hate all who do wrong" (Ps. 5:4–5, NIV).

Lord, You have instructed Your followers to "depart from evil and do good; seek peace and pursue it" (Ps. 34:14, NKJV). I have committed my life to following Your instructions, Lord.

Father, You have told Your followers, "Don't worry about the wicked or envy those who do wrong. For like grass, they soon fade away. Like spring flowers, they soon wither" (Ps. 37:1–2, NLT).

Father, I will be still in Your presence and wait patiently for You to act. I will not worry about evil people who prosper, and I will not fret about their wicked schemes (Ps. 37:7, NKJV).

Father, I am so thankful for Your Word, which promises, "It is better to be godly and have little than to be evil and rich. For the strength of the wicked will be shattered, but the LORD takes care of the godly. Day by day the LORD takes care of the innocent, and they will receive an inheritance that lasts forever. They will not be disgraced in hard times; even in famine they will have more than enough. But the wicked will die. The LORD's enemies are like flowers in a field—they will disappear like smoke" (Ps. 37:16–20, NLT).

Father, I will obey Your Word to "turn from evil and do good, and you will live in the land forever. For the LORD loves justice, and he will never abandon the godly" (Ps. 37:27–28, NLT).

Lord, "The wicked wait in ambush for the godly, looking for an excuse to kill them. But the LORD will not let the wicked succeed or let the godly be condemned when they are put on trial" (Ps. 37:32–33, NLT).

Father, just like the psalmist David, I see the evil in our land, and I know that You will cause the plans of evildoers to fail. Like David, I say to the evildoers, "You people may be strong and brag about your sins, but God can be trusted day after day. You plan brutal crimes, and your lying words cut like a sharp razor. You would rather do evil than good, and tell lies than speak the truth. You love to say cruel things, and your words are a trap. God will destroy you forever! He will grab you and drag you from your homes. You will be uprooted and left to die. When good people see this fearsome sight, they will laugh and say, 'Just look at them now! Instead of trusting God, they trusted their wealth and their cruelty'" (Ps. 52:1–7, CEV).

Lord, at times it seems like the evil plans and schemes of men and women who are living godless lives will succeed, and Your children will suffer because of them. But I am committing myself to taking a stand on Your Word. I stand in agreement with Psalm 91, and I will:

1. Live under Your protection and stay in Your shadow

2. Proclaim that You are my fortress and place of safety

3. Believe You are my God and trust You

4. Trust that You will keep me safe from secret traps and deadly diseases

5. Be safe and secure under Your wings

6. Have no fear of dangers at night or in the

daytime, because Your faithfulness is like a shield and a city wall

7. Have faith that no disease will strike in the night and no disasters will come in the daytime

8. Know that though thousands fall to danger around me, I will not be harmed

9. See You punish the wicked with my own eyes, and I will run to You for safety

10. Experience no terrible disasters striking my home, my family, or me

11. Believe that You have commanded Your angels to protect me wherever I go

12. Declare that Your power will be stronger than the strongest lions or the most deadly snakes

13. Be safe because I love You and serve You

14. Call on You when I am in trouble, and You will protect and honor me

15. Live a long life and live to see Your saving power

Father, sometimes unjust leaders boldly claim that God is on their side, yet they are leaders who permit injustice. They gang up on the righteous and condemn the innocent to death through their unjust laws and regulations. But when this happens, You are my fortress and the mighty rock on which I stand. You have promised to turn their sins back upon them and destroy them in the way they planned to destroy Your children (Ps. 94:20–23, NKJV).

Father, in this day when it seems that godless men and godless laws are destroying the godly life and foundations on which this nation was founded, Your Word brings courage and strength to Your people. In it You have promised that our "children will be successful everywhere," and "an entire generation of godly people will be blessed." Your people will possess wealth, and our good deeds will last forever. "Light shines in the darkness for the godly." Your people will be "generous, compassionate, and righteous." Good will come to those who lend money generously and conduct business fairly. We will not be overcome by evil. As we confidently trust in You to care for us, we will be confident and fearless and face our foes triumphantly. We will have influence and honor, and when the wicked see this, it will infuriate them. They will grind their teeth in anger and slink away as their hopes are thwarted (Ps. 112, NLT).

Father, You have promised, "Whoever listens to me will dwell safely, and will be secure, without fear of evil" (Prov. 1:33, NKJV).

Father, You have warned Your children, "Do not

enter the path of the wicked, and do not walk in the way of evil" (Prov. 4:14, NKJV).

Father, You have counseled Your children, "Do not turn to the right or the left; remove your foot from evil" (Prov. 4:27, NKJV).

Father, Your Word promises, "No grave trouble will overtake the righteous, but the wicked shall be filled with evil" (Prov. 12:21, NKJV).

Father, "a wise man fears and departs from evil, but a fool rages and is self-confident" (Prov. 14:16, NKJV).

Father, help me to carefully consider what I say and to be sure my answers are godly and truthful. You have said, "The heart of the righteous studies how to answer, but the mouth of the wicked pours forth evil" (Prov. 15:28, NKJV).

PRAYER AGAINST EVIL

"O LORD, rescue me from evil people. Protect me from those who are violent, those who plot evil in their hearts and stir up trouble all day long. Their tongues sting like a snake; the venom of a viper drips from their lips. O LORD, keep me out of the hands of the wicked. Protect me from those who are violent, for they are plotting against me. The proud have set a trap to catch me; they have stretched out a net; they have placed traps all along the way. I said to the LORD, 'You are my God!' Listen, O LORD, to my cries for mercy! O Sovereign LORD, the strong one who rescued me, you protected me on the day of battle. LORD, do not let evil people have their way. Do not let their evil schemes succeed, or they will become proud. Let my enemies be destroyed by the very evil they have planned for me. Let burning coals fall down on their heads. Let them be thrown into the fire or into watery pits from which they can't escape. Don't let liars prosper here in our land. Cause great disasters to fall on the violent. But I know the LORD will help those they persecute; he will give justice to the poor. Surely righteous people are praising your name; the godly will live in your presence" (Ps. 140, NLT).

CHAPTER 9

THE CURSE OF UNGODLY SOUL TIES AND GODLESSNESS

Do not be unequally yoked together with unbe-
lievers. For what fellowship has righteousness with
lawlessness? And what communion has light with
darkness? And what accord has Christ with Belial?
Or what part has a believer with an unbeliever?
—2 Corinthians 6:14–15, NKJV

WHEN THERE IS an unequal yoke between believers and unbelievers, we call this an *ungodly soul tie*. Breaking ungodly soul ties is a key to deliverance. Ungodly association causes evil spirits to be transferred. If Belial cannot directly control you, he will influence you through ungodly association.

Associating with the wrong people can cause you to receive an *evil transfer* of spirits. One of the keys to being delivered from Belial's control is to break every ungodly soul tie and to obey the Word of God, which says, "Do not be unequally yoked together with unbelievers" (2 Cor. 6:14, NKJV). The Amplified Bible says, "Do not be unequally yoked with unbelievers [do not make mismated alliances with them or come under a different yoke with them, inconsistent with your faith]."

This is the only time the name Belial is mentioned in the New Testament. I believe the Spirit of God chose this word to bring revelation to a spirit that the church *must not in any way* be in fellowship with.

Verse 15 ties Belial with unrighteousness, darkness, infidels, and idolatry. The first reference to Belial in the Word of God ties him to *idolatry*. The Corinthians had been saved from a lifestyle of idolatry.

As stated before, I believe that Belial is an End Time spirit who will be an enemy of the church. We are to separate ourselves from all uncleanness and filthiness that is associated with this ruling spirit.

The church at Corinth also had a problem with carnality. There were strife, envy, contention, sexual impurity, and even drunkenness taking place within the church. The apostle Paul wrote the letter to Corinth to correct these problems and to set things in order.

A FLOOD OF UNGODLINESS

When the waves of death surrounded me, the floods of ungodliness made me afraid.

—2 Samuel 22:5, NKJV

The literal translation of this verse is "...the floods of Belial." This verse is a portion of a song David sang in the day the Lord delivered him out of the hands of all his enemies and out of the hand of Saul.

The American Standard Version says, "The floods of ungodliness made me afraid." Belial has released a flood of ungodliness upon our nation. *Ungodly* is defined as "denying God or being disobedient to Him: impious, irreligious, contrary to moral law, sinful, wicked."

Belial is responsible for the flood of ungodliness manifested through Hollywood, television, and the mass media. Belial is responsible for rebellion and disobedience to God. This spirit has cursed many, causing them to be irreligious and impious.

Having no reverence—no fear of God—is the result of Belial's influence. *To flood* means "to cover, to inundate, to fill abundantly or excessively." Belial desires to cover the earth with filth and immorality. This flood also includes the persecution that comes against the Lord's anointed, David.

Belial desires to murder and destroy the Lord's anointed. He is a strongman who attacks ministers and churches. The New American Standard Bible says, "The torrents of destruction overwhelmed me." We find that the word *torrent* is defined as "an outpouring, a rush."

Perdition means "destruction." Spirits of *death and destruction* work with Belial to assail the servants of God. We have already seen that Jezebel works under Belial to destroy true servants of God. Lies, slander, seduction, lust, and pride are all weapons used against the Lord's anointed.

It is important to intercede against Belial's curses. When the enemy shall come in like a flood, the Spirit of the Lord will lift up a standard against him. The Lord will lift up a standard against the floods of Belial. The prayers and intercessions of God's people will be a standard against this flood.

Coming Against Belial

But the sons of Belial shall be all of them as thorns thrust away, because they cannot be taken with hands: but the man that shall touch them must be fenced with iron and the staff of a spear; and they shall be utterly burned with fire in the same place.
—2 Samuel 23:6–7

This verse compares the "sons of Belial" to thorns that cannot be handled. Those who deal with Belial "must be fenced with iron and the staff of a spear." A *thorn* is something that causes distress or irritation. *To be thorny* means "to be full of difficulties or controversial points."

This verse pronounces the judgment upon Belial and those who follow him: "They shall be utterly burned with fire in the same place." This is a reference to eternal damnation in hellfire. I believe that Belial is a spirit that will cause many to die lost and spend eternity in hell.

"Fenced with iron and the staff of a spear" is a reference

to putting on the whole armor of God. We cannot deal with this spirit without the whole armor of God.

The Lord is raising up intercessors and preachers to come against this spirit in the last days. This is an End Time spirit assigned to corrupt the earth, but the Lord has an *End Time people* to combat him. Young's Literal Translation says, "And the man who cometh against them...."

David had to fight and overcome the men controlled by Belial. David is a type of the New Testament church. He is a type of the prophetic church the Lord is raising up in this hour. Just as David overcame, we will also overcome this End Time spirit.

We will not handle this spirit with our natural hands. He is too thorny and difficult for that. But we must and will attack him in the power of the Spirit, wearing the whole armor of God.

PRAYERS

SEPARATION FROM BELIAL

Father, You have instructed us, "Do not be unequally yoked together with unbelievers. For what fellowship has righteousness with lawlessness? And what communion has light with darkness? And what accord has Christ with Belial? Or what part has a believer with an unbeliever? And what agreement has the temple of God with idols? For you are the temple of the living God.... Therefore come out from among them and be separate.... Do not touch what is unclean, and I will receive you" (2 Cor. 6:14–17, NKJV).

Father, You have stressed how important it is to guard our hearts from evil by saying, "Keep and guard your heart with all vigilance and above all that you guard, for out of it flow the springs of life" (Prov. 4:23, AMP).

Father, help us to remember Your Word: "God's will is for you to be holy, so stay away from all sexual sin. Then each of you will control his own body and live in holiness and honor—not in lustful passion like the pagans who do not know God and his ways.... God has called us to live holy lives, not impure lives" (1 Thess. 4:3–5, 7, NLT).

Father, help us to remember to guard our souls by refusing to be united to anything that is evil, for Your Word tells us, "Beloved, I implore you as aliens and strangers and exiles [in this world] to abstain from the sensual urges (the evil desires, the passions of the flesh, your lower nature) that wage war against the soul" (1 Pet. 2:11, AMP).

GUARD YOUR SOUL

Father, I have committed myself to: "Love the LORD your God with all your heart and with all your soul and with all your strength" (Deut. 6:5, NIV).

Lord, it is for my own good that You have asked me to love You with all my heart *and all my soul.* For You have said, "What does the LORD your God ask of you but to fear the LORD your God, to walk in all his ways, to love him, to serve the LORD your God with all your heart and with all your soul, and to observe the LORD's commands and decrees that I am giving you today for your own good?" (Deut. 10:12–13, NIV).

Father, Your Word warns us of the dangers that can come because of deep soul ties. You have said, "If your brother, the son of your mother, your son or your daughter, the wife of your bosom, or your friend *who is as your own soul,* secretly entices you, saying, 'Let us go and serve other gods,' which you have not known…you shall not consent to him or listen to him, nor shall your eye pity him, nor shall you spare him or conceal him; but you shall surely kill him; your hand shall be first against him to put him to death, and afterward the hand of all the people. And you shall stone him with stones until he dies, because he sought to entice you away from the LORD your God, who brought you out of the land of Egypt, from the house of bondage" (Deut. 13:6, 8–10, NKJV, emphasis added).

Lord, You have told me, "Now devote your heart and soul to seeking the LORD your God" (1 Chron. 22:19, NIV). May I always remember that if I allow my soul to be unguarded and develop a deep soul tie with an unbeliever, it could separate me from You.

Father, You warn us that our soul can be trapped by anger, and You say, "Make no friendship with an angry man, and with a furious man do not go, lest you learn his ways and set a snare for your soul" (Prov. 22:24–25, NKJV). Keep me from binding my soul to anger.

Father, we live in a world where many have lost their hope because of desperate situations and rampant godlessness. Yet Your Word promises how our souls can be constantly filled with hope for the future. You tell us in Your Word, "Eat honey, my son, for it is good; honey from the comb is sweet to your taste. Know also that wisdom is sweet to your soul; if you find it, there is a future hope for you, and your hope will not be cut off" (Prov. 24:13–14, NIV).

Father, teach me to remember that my soul must be filled with Your goodness—not with things of this world. You have told us, "Why spend money on

PRAYERS ᴛꞰ႐ᴛ BꞀ℮Ⴍᴋ CURSES

what is not bread, and your labor on what does not
satisfy? Listen, listen to me, and eat what is good,
and your soul will delight in the richest of fare"
(Prov. 55:2, NIV).

Father, when we find that our hearts and souls are
weary and bound by cares and unhealthy soul ties,
then we must "stand in the ways and see, and ask
for the old paths, where the good way is, and walk
in it; then you will find rest for your souls" (Jer.
6:16, NKJV).

Lord, teach me to respect the spiritual leaders You
have placed over me, as You have instructed in
Your Word: "Obey those who rule over you, and
be submissive, for they watch out for your souls, as
those who must give account. Let them do so with
joy and not with grief, for that would be unprofit-
able for you" (Heb. 13:17, NKJV).

UNGODLINESS

Lord, Your servant David came to a time in his
life when he felt as though he were drowning in a
flood of enemies who were trying to destroy him,
yet You rescued him. I pray that You will rescue
me from the floodwaters of trouble, and I too will
praise You, as David praised You. "Our LORD and
our God, you are my mighty rock, my fortress, my

protector. You are the rock where I am safe. You are my shield, my powerful weapon, and my place of shelter. You rescue me and keep me from being hurt. I praise you, our LORD! I prayed to you, and you rescued me from my enemies. Death, like ocean waves, surrounded me, and I was almost swallowed by its flooding waters. Ropes from the world of the dead had coiled around me, and death had set a trap in my path. I was in terrible trouble when I called out to you, but from your temple you heard me and answered my prayer....You roared at the sea, and its deepest channels....You reached down from heaven, and you lifted me from deep in the ocean. You rescued me from enemies who were hateful and too powerful for me....Only you are a mighty rock" (2 Sam. 22:1–7, 16–18, 32, CEV). You are my strong fortress, and You set me free.

Father, when the flood of sin and ungodliness threatens my life and my family, I will call upon You as David did and proclaim, "The voice of the LORD echoes over the oceans. The glorious LORD God thunders above the roar of the raging sea, and his voice is mighty and marvelous....The LORD rules on his throne, king of the flood forever. Pray that our LORD will make us strong and give us peace" (Ps. 29:3–4, 10–11, CEV).

"Save me, God! I am about to drown. I am sinking

99

deep in the mud, and my feet are slipping. I am about to be swept under by a mighty flood.... But I pray to you, LORD. So when the time is right, answer me and help me with your wonderful love. Don't let me sink in the mud, but save me from my enemies and from the deep water. Don't let me be swept away by a flood or drowned in the ocean or swallowed by death. Answer me, LORD! You are kind and good" (Ps. 69:1–2, 13–16, CEV).

Father, I am not afraid of the flood of unrighteousness and ungodliness that is rising in our nation. I know that You will save Your people, just as You promise in Your Word: "By your power you made a path through the sea, and you smashed the heads of sea monsters. You crushed the heads of the monster Leviathan, then fed him to wild creatures in the desert. You opened the ground for streams and springs and dried up mighty rivers. You rule the day and the night, and you put the moon and the sun in place.... Violent enemies are hiding in every dark corner of the earth. Don't disappoint those in need or make them turn from you, but help the poor and homeless to shout your praises" (Ps. 74:13–16, 20–21, CEV).

Father, I will not fear the flood of ungodliness in our nation, for Your Word promises, "Now the LORD will get furious and do to his enemies, both near and far, what they did to his people. He will attack like a flood in a mighty windstorm. Nations in the west and the east will then honor and praise his wonderful name" (Isa. 59:18–19, CEV).

Lord, the day will come when You will come in a flood of godliness and power, and all the floodwaters of sin and ungodliness will give way to the fresh floods of glory and power from You. Your Word prophesies, "And it will come to pass in that day that the mountains shall drip with new wine, the hills shall flow with milk, and all the brooks of Judah shall be flooded with water; a fountain shall flow from the house of the LORD and water the Valley of Acacias.... For the LORD dwells in Zion" (Joel 3:18, 21, NKJV).

Lord, I want my life to be built upon the strong rock of Jesus Christ, for then when the flood of ungodliness sweeps in, I will be like the wise man who built his house on the rock: "And the rain descended, the floods came, and the winds blew and beat on that house; and it did not fall, for it was founded on the rock" (Matt. 7:25, NKJV).

AVOIDING UNGODLINESS

Father, You give us the steps to follow to avoid being snared by ungodliness: "Be diligent to present

PRAYERS T ̄OT BⱣƐQK CURSES

yourself approved to God, a worker who does not need to be ashamed, rightly dividing the word of truth. But shun profane and idle babblings, for they will increase to more ungodliness" (2 Tim. 2:15–16, NKJV).

Lord, help me to follow the advice that the apostle Paul gave his young helper Timothy: "You therefore, my son, be strong in the grace that is in Christ Jesus. And the things that you have heard from me among many witnesses, commit these to faithful men who will be able to teach others also. You therefore must endure hardship as a good soldier of Jesus Christ. No one engaged in warfare entangles himself with the affairs of this life, that he may please him who enlisted him as a soldier" (2 Tim. 2:1–4, NKJV).

Father, the apostle Paul listed the steps that You have taken to ensure that Your followers do not fall into ungodliness. I praise You for these blessings (Eph. 1:3–14, NKJV):

1. Blessed be the God and Father of our Lord Jesus Christ, who has blessed us with every spiritual blessing in the heavenly places in Christ.

2. He chose us in Him before the foundation of the world, that we should be holy and without blame before Him in love.

3. He predestined us to adoption as sons by Jesus

Christ to Himself, according to the good pleasure of His will.

4. He made us accepted in the Beloved.

5. In Him we have redemption through His blood,
the forgiveness of sins, according to the riches
of His grace, which He made to abound toward
us in all wisdom and prudence.

6. He made known to us the mystery of His will,
according to His good pleasure, which He
purposed in Himself.

7. In Him also we have obtained an inheritance,
being predestined according to the purpose
of Him who works all things according to the
counsel of His will.

8. In Him you also trusted, after you heard the
word of truth, the gospel of your salvation; in
whom also, having believed, you were sealed
with the Holy Spirit of promise.

9. He is the guarantee of our inheritance until the
redemption of the purchased possession, to the
praise of His glory.

Father, just as Paul prayed for the believers at
Philippi, I pray for my fellow believers, that we
may not fall into ungodliness. "I thank my God
upon every remembrance of you, always in every
prayer of mine making request for you all with

joy, for your fellowship in the gospel from the first day until now, being confident of this very thing, that He who has begun a good work in you will complete it until the day of Jesus Christ.... And this I pray, that your love may abound still more and more in knowledge and all discernment, that you may approve the things that are excellent, that you may be sincere and without offense till the day of Christ, being filled with the fruits of righteousness which are by Jesus Christ, to the glory and praise of God" (Phil. 1:3–6, 9–11, NKJV).

Lord, "blessed is the man who walks not in the counsel of the ungodly, nor stands in the path of sinners, nor sits in the seat of the scornful; but his delight is in the law of the LORD, and in His law he meditates day and night. He shall be like a tree planted by the rivers of water, that brings forth its fruit in its season, whose leaf also shall not wither; and whatever he does shall prosper" (Ps. 1:1–3).

CHAPTER 10

WICKED PLOTS AGAINST the GODLY

*An ungodly man digs up evil, and it is
on his lips like a burning fire.*
—Proverbs 16:27, NKJV

THE AMERICAN STANDARD Version says, "A worthless man deviseth mischief." The Contemporary English Version says, "Worthless people plan trouble." *To devise* means "to plan to bring about." A *plot* is a secret plan, usually for accomplishing an evil or unlawful end.

Belial causes men to plan and plot evil. Psalm 37:12 says, "The wicked plots against the just" (NKJV). There are people involved in forms of witchcraft that are planning to destroy the church. We have heard reports of witches fasting to break up marriages of Christian leaders and to disrupt the church.

It is almost hard to believe that there are actually people this wicked. I believe it because the Word of God states it.

Most people would be shocked to know the types of gross sins and plots taking place behind closed doors.

Psalm 37:32 says, "The wicked watches the righteous, and seeks to slay him" (NKJV). The Amplified Version says, "The wicked lie in wait for the [uncompromisingly] righteous and seek to put them to death." The New Living Translation says, "The wicked wait in ambush for the godly, looking for an excuse to kill them."

What a sobering thought! No wonder the Word of God admonishes us to be *sober and vigilant*. Belial will influence men to plot against the righteous.

CURSING THE LORD'S ANOINTED

> And when king David came to Bahurim, behold, thence came out a man of the family of the house of Saul, whose name was Shimei, the son of Gera: he came forth, and cursed still as he came. And he cast stones at David, and at all the servants of king David: and all the people and all the mighty men were on his right hand and on his left. And thus said Shimei when he cursed, Come out, come out, thou bloody man, and thou man of Belial.
>
> —2 Samuel 16:5–7

Shimei was calling David a worthless man. The Contemporary English Version says, "...you good-for-nothing." David was fleeing from his rebellious son, Absalom, when he encountered Shimei. Shimei was from the family of the house of Saul and was no doubt angry at the fact that David had succeeded Saul as king. This is just like the enemy to accuse God's anointed.

The Pharisees said Jesus cast out devils by Beelzebub. They were accusing Him of using Satan's power to deliver people. To call someone a "man of Belial" is to call that person worthless, no good, wicked, base, and vile. Shimei was accusing David of being a rebellious murderer who was responsible for Saul's fall. This is another example of how this spirit will attack and accuse the Lord's anointed.

> But Abishai the son of Zeruiah answered and said, "Shall not Shimei be put to death for this, *because he cursed the Lord's anointed*?"
> —2 Samuel 19:21, NKJV, emphasis added

After David was returned to his position in Jerusalem, Shimei came to him and repented of what he said. Abishai desired to have him put to death for cursing the Lord's anointed. David, however, had mercy upon Shimei and did not put him to death.

David understood the judgment that would come upon those who touched the Lord's anointed. He refused to touch Saul, even though his life was in danger. In the case of Shimei, mercy prevailed over judgment because of Shimei's *repentant* attitude.

Strong intercessors help cover the men and women of

God from the attacks of Belial. A *curse* is an evil work spoken against a person or a thing. Words spoken against the servants of God are spiritual arrows sent by the enemy to hurt and destroy. They are what the Word refers to as the "fiery darts of the wicked" (Eph. 6:16, NKJV).

David understood the spiritual warfare the Lord's anointed must face when men curse. David prays in Psalm 64:2–3, "Hide me from the secret counsel of the wicked; from the insurrection of the workers of iniquity. Who whet their tongue like a sword, and bend their bows to shoot their arrows, even bitter words."

These words are *witchcraft attacks* against the servants of the Lord. They are spiritual missiles directed toward the Lord's anointed. Life and death are in the power of the tongue (Prov. 18:21). This is one of the methods Belial uses to direct his assault against the servants of the Lord.

PRAYERS

PLOTS OF THE WICKED

Father, in their prideful, sinning ways, the wicked create plots to destroy the righteous. But You have promised, "The wicked in his pride persecutes the poor; let them be caught in the plots which they have devised" (Ps. 10:2, NKJV).

Lord, the wicked plot continually to cause trouble and destruction to Your children. Your Word says that the wicked "sits in the lurking places of the villages; in the secret places he murders the innocent; his eyes are secretly fixed on the helpless" (Ps. 10:8, NKJV). Lord, this describes the wicked plans of people today to spread the pain and sin of abortion. Shine the light of Your judgments upon the secretive, liberal attempts to lure young girls into a decision to abort the precious lives they are carrying. Stop the murder of the unborn, and cast this evil practice out of America.

Lord, Your Word describes the secret agenda of ungodly liberals to bind the poor into a lifestyle of dependence on others rather than independence and self-reliance. Your Word says, "He lies in wait secretly, as a lion in his den; he lies in wait to catch the poor; he catches the poor when he draws him into his net. So he crouches, he lies low, that the helpless may fall by his strength" (Ps. 10:9–10, NKJV). Give us courage as Americans to become self-reliant, self-confident, and willing to be responsible for ourselves if possible rather than dependent on others.

Lord, like the writer of Proverbs, I feel as though I am being destroyed by the wicked plots of those who want to hurt me. But, like Solomon, my prayer is directed to You for Your grace and mercy: "I trust you, LORD, and I claim you as my God. My life is in your hands. Save me from enemies who hunt me down. Smile on me, your servant. Have pity and rescue me. I pray only to you. Don't disappoint me. Disappoint my cruel enemies until they lie silent in their graves. Silence those proud liars! Make them stop bragging and insulting your people. You are wonderful, and while everyone watches, you store up blessings for all who honor and trust. You are their shelter from harmful plots, and you are their protection from vicious gossip. I will praise you, LORD, for showing great kindness when I was like a city under attack. I was terrified and thought, 'They've chased me far away from you!' But you answered my prayer when I shouted for help. All who belong to the LORD, show how you love him. The LORD protects the faithful, but he severely punishes everyone who is proud. All who trust the LORD, be cheerful and strong" (Ps. 31:14–24, CEV).

THE WICKED WAR AGAINST THE GODLY

Lord, sometimes I feel just like David—surrounded by wickedness and threatened by destruction of my life. David cried out, saying, "Enemies are all around like a herd of wild bulls.…My enemies are like lions roaring and attacking with jaws open wide. I have no more strength than a few drops of water. All my bones are out of joint; my heart is like melted wax. My strength has dried up like a broken clay pot, and my tongue sticks to the roof of my mouth. You, God, have left me to die in the dirt. Brutal enemies attack me like a pack of dogs, tearing at my hands and my feet. I can count all my bones, and my enemies just stare and sneer at me.... Don't stay far away, LORD!" (Ps. 22:12–17, 19, CEV). But, like David, I know this one thing: "My strength comes from you, so hurry and help" (v. 20).

David knew that You would come to his help, Lord, and so do I. I will follow the advice of Your Word: "Be patient and trust the LORD. Don't let it bother you when all goes well for those who do sinful things. Don't be angry or furious. Anger can lead to sin. All sinners will disappear, but if you trust the LORD, the land will be yours" (Ps. 37:7–9, CEV).

Father, Your Word describes a wicked person: "A worthless person, a wicked man, walks with a perverse mouth; he winks with his eyes, he shuffles his feet, he points with his fingers; perversity is in his heart, he devises evil continually, he sows discord. Therefore his calamity shall come suddenly; suddenly he shall be broken without remedy. These six things the LORD hates, yes, seven are an abomination to Him: a proud look, a lying tongue, hands that shed innocent blood, a heart that devises wicked plans, feet that are swift in running to evil, a false witness who speaks lies, and one who sows discord among brethren" (Prov. 6:12–19, NKJV).

Father, I will strengthen my heart by praying these words from David: "Rescue me from cruel and violent enemies, LORD! They think up evil plans and always cause trouble. Their words bite deep like the poisonous fangs of a snake. Protect me, LORD, from cruel and brutal enemies who want to destroy me. Those proud people have hidden traps and nets to catch me as I walk. You, LORD, are my God! Please listen to my prayer. You have the power to save me, and you keep me safe in every battle. Don't let the wicked succeed in doing what they want, or else they might never stop planning evil. They have me surrounded, but make them the victims of their own vicious lies. Dump flaming coals on them and throw them into pits where they can't climb out. Chase those cruel liars away! Let trouble hunt them down. Our LORD, I know that you defend the homeless and see that the poor are given justice. Your people will praise you and will live with you because they do right" (Ps. 140, CEV).

GOD PROTECTS HIS ANOINTED

Father, even when David was being pursued by Saul, he refused to do anything that would harm Saul, who was Your anointed king over Israel. After he cut off a piece of Saul's robe in the cave, he stopped his men from hurting Saul, because Saul was the anointed servant of God: "And David arose and secretly cut off a corner of Saul's robe. Now it happened afterward that David's heart troubled him because he had cut Saul's robe. And he said to his men, 'The LORD forbid that I should do this thing to my master, the LORD's anointed, to stretch out my hand against him, seeing he is the anointed of the LORD.' So David restrained his servants with these words, and did not allow them to rise against Saul. And Saul got up from the cave and went on his way" (1 Sam. 24:4–7, NKJV).

Father, again another time when David and Abishai stood before Saul as he slept, Abishai said, "'God has delivered your enemy into your hand this day. Now therefore, please, let me strike him at once with the spear, right to the earth; and I will not have to strike him a second time!' But David said to Abishai, 'Do not destroy him; for who can stretch out his hand against the LORD's anointed, and be guiltless?' David said furthermore, 'As the LORD lives, the LORD shall strike him, or his day shall come to die, or he shall go out to battle and perish. The LORD forbid that I should stretch out my hand against the LORD's anointed. But please, take now the spear and the jug of water that are by his head, and let us go.' So David took the spear and the jug of water by Saul's head, and they got away; and no man saw or knew it or awoke" (1 Sam. 26:8–12, NKJV). Father, help me to honor Your anointed servants just as David honored Saul.

Lord, when You made a covenant with Abraham, Isaac, and Jacob, You included this warning as a part of Your covenant: "Do not touch My anointed ones, and do My prophets no harm" (1 Chron. 16:22, NKJV). May I always remember the value you place on Your anointed servants, and may I never do or say anything to dishonor them or to harm them.

Lord, Your Word promises, "Now I know that the LORD saves His anointed; He will answer him from His holy heaven with the saving strength of His right hand" (Ps. 20:6).

Father, David recognized that he was anointed by You and that You were the source of his strength. He praised You with these words: "The LORD is my strength and my shield; My heart trusted in Him, and I am helped; therefore my heart greatly rejoices, and with my song I will praise Him. The

L ORD is their strength, and He is the saving refuge of His anointed. Save Your people, and bless Your inheritance; shepherd them also, and bear them up forever" (Ps. 28:7–9).

CHAPTER 11

LOOSE YOURSELF FROM BELIAL'S CURSES

*Verily I say unto you, Whatsoever ye shall bind
on earth shall be bound in heaven: and whatsoever
ye shall loose on earth shall be loosed in heaven.*
—Matthew 18:18

*Shake thyself from the dust; arise, and sit down,
O Jerusalem: loose thyself from the bands of
thy neck, O captive daughter of Zion.*
—Isaiah 52:2

THIS IS A prophetic word to the church that says, "Loose thyself!" It is a powerful verse that relates to self-deliverance. We have been given the power and authority to loose ourselves from all types of bondage.

The word *loose* means "to disjoin, to divorce, to separate, asunder, sever, unhitch, disconnect, detach, unseat, unbind, unchain, unfetter, free, release, liberate, break up, break in pieces, smash, shatter, splinter, demolish, cleave, force apart." It also means "to forgive or pardon."

Zion is a prophetic word and symbol for the church. Isaiah prophesied that Zion would be a "captive daughter." This is so true of the condition of the church today. Even though many are saved and have received the promise of the Spirit, there are still many bondages that remain in the lives of believers.

SELF-DELIVERANCE

The question is often asked of me, "Can a person deliver himself of demons?" My answer is yes. It is also my conviction that a person cannot really keep himself free of demons until he is walking in this dimension of deliverance.

How is it that a person can deliver himself? As a believer (and that is our assumption), a person has the same authority as the believer who is ministering deliverance to another. He has the authority in the name of Jesus, and Jesus plainly promised those who believe, "In my name shall they cast out devils" (Mark 16:17).

Usually a person needs only to learn how to go about performing self-deliverance. After a person has experienced an initial deliverance at the hands of an experienced minister, he can begin to practice self-deliverance.*

The good news is that we have been given a prophetic promise and a command to loose ourselves. Jesus told His disciples that "whatsoever" we loose on Earth is loosed in heaven.

Whatsoever is binding, harassing, or operating in your life contrary to the will of God can be loosed from your life because you have been given the authority to do so.

The range of things that can bind a believer is almost limitless. There are many bondages we can categorize that need to be exposed and broken in the lives of all believers. Once you identify the enemy, you can then proceed to free yourself from his clutches.

LOOSE THYSELF FROM THE PAST

I have ministered to many believers who are still bound and tied to their past. The *past* can be a chain that keeps you from enjoying the present and being successful in the future.

While ministering deliverance to a young man, a strong spirit manifested who boasted that he would not depart. I commanded the spirit to identify himself, and he replied that his name was Past.

---

* See Frank Hammond, *Pigs in the Parlor* (Kirkwood, MO: Impact Christian Books, 1973), 57.

The spirit proceeded to explain that it was his job to keep the young man bound to his past so that he could not be successful in his Christian walk. The young man had been through a divorce, and his past continued to haunt him.

This encounter helped to give me a revelation of the fact that there are numerous spirits assigned to people to keep them bound to the past that have left scars and wounds that have not completely healed. Many of these wounds have been infected and have become the dwelling places of unclean spirits. People need to be loosed not only from demons but also from other people. Ungodly soul ties are avenues spirits of control and manipulation utilize when working upon their unwary victims.

PRAYER FOR DELIVERANCE

Father, in Jesus's name, I loose myself from all relationships that are not ordained of God; all relationships that are not of the Spirit but of the flesh; all relationships based on control, domination, or manipulation; and all relationships based on lust and deception.

In the name of Jesus, I loose all members of my body, including my mind, memory, eyes, ears, tongue, hands, feet, and my entire sexual character, from all lust, perversion, sexual impurity, uncleanness, lasciviousness, promiscuity, pornography, fornication, homosexuality, fantasy, filthiness, burning passion, and uncontrollable sex drive.

I loose myself from the effects of all bad memories, painful memories, and memories of the past that would hinder me in the present or future.

I loose myself from all occult involvement, all sorcery, divination, witchcraft, psychic inheritance, rebellion, all confusion, sickness, death, and destruction as a result of occult involvement.

In the name of the Lord Jesus Christ, by the authority given to me to bind and loose, I loose my emotions from every evil spirit that has come in as a result of experiences of the past. I loose myself from all hurt, deep hurt, pain, sadness, grief, anger, hatred, rage, bitterness, fear, and bound and blocked emotions. I command these spirits to come out, and I decree freedom to my emotions in the name of Jesus.

I loose my mind from all spirits of mind control, confusion, mental bondage, insanity, madness, fantasy, passivity, intellectualism, knowledge block, ignorance, mind binding, lust, and evil thinking. I loose myself from all guilt, shame, condemnation, self-condemnation, and legalism.

I loose my will from all control domination and manipulation from Satan, his demons, and other people. I loose my will from all lust, rebellion, stubbornness, pride, self-will, selfishness, and antisubmissive spirits that block and hinder my will. I break and loose myself from all chains around my will, and I submit my will to the will of God.

CHAPTER 12

SAFE FROM the CURSE of BELIAL

The path of the just is like the shining sun,
that shines ever brighter unto the perfect day.
The way of the wicked is like darkness; they
do not know what makes them stumble.
—Proverbs 4:18–19, NKJV

FATHER, MAY I always remember the lessons You teach us in Proverbs 10, as You contrast the blessings for the righteous with the punishments for the wicked. These are Your promises to the righteous—and Your warnings to the wicked.

(Note: make a commitment to meditate each day of the coming month on one of these promises/punishments adapted from Proverbs 10, NKJV.)

1. The Lord will not allow the righteous soul to famish, but He casts away the desire of the wicked.

2. He who has a slack hand becomes poor, but the hand of the diligent makes rich.

3. He who gathers in the summer is a wise son; he who sleeps in harvest is a son who causes shame.

4. Blessings are on the head of the righteous, but violence covers the mouth of the wicked.

5. The memory of the righteous is blessed, but the name of the wicked will rot.

6. The wise in heart will receive commands, but a prating fool will fall.

7. He who walks with integrity walks securely, but he who perverts his ways will become known.

8. He who winks with the eye causes trouble, but a prating fool will fall.

9. The mouth of the righteous is a well of life, but violence covers the mouth of the wicked.

10. Hatred stirs up strife, but love covers all sins.

11. Wisdom is found on the lips of him who has understanding, but a rod is for the back of him who is devoid of understanding.

12. Wise people store up knowledge, but the mouth of the foolish is near destruction.

13. The rich man's wealth is his strong city; the destruction of the poor is their poverty.

14. The labor of the righteous leads to life; the wages of the wicked, to sin.

15. He who keeps instruction is in the way of life, but he who refuses correction goes astray.

16. Whoever hides hatred has lying lips, and whoever spreads slander is a fool.

17. In the multitude of words sin is not lacking, but he who restrains his lips is wise.

18. The tongue of the righteous is choice silver; the heart of the wicked is worth little.

19. The lips of the righteous feed many, but fools die for lack of wisdom.

20. The blessing of the Lord makes one rich, and He adds no sorrow with it.

21. To do evil is like sport to a fool, but a man of understanding has wisdom.

22. The fear of the wicked will come upon him, and the desire of the righteous will be granted.

23. When the whirlwind passes by, the wicked is no more, but the righteous has an everlasting foundation.

24. As vinegar to the teeth and smoke to the eyes, so is the lazy man to those who send him.

25. The fear of the Lord prolongs days, but the years of the wicked will be shortened.

26. The hope of the righteous will be gladness, but the expectation of the wicked will perish.

27. The way of the Lord is strength for the upright, but destruction will come to the workers of iniquity.

28. The righteous will never be removed, but the wicked will not inhabit the earth.

29. The mouth of the righteous brings forth wisdom, but the perverse tongue will be cut out.

30. The lips of the righteous know what is acceptable, but the mouth of the wicked what is perverse.

The remaining chapters of Proverbs contain many more of these contrasted blessings for the righteous and punishments for the wicked. As an additional Bible study on righteousness contrasted with wickedness, continue selecting one contrast each day as your focus topic verse and prayer subject.

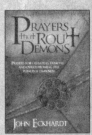
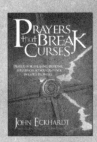

FREE NEWSLETTERS
TO HELP EMPOWER YOUR LIFE

Why subscribe today?

☐ **DELIVERED DIRECTLY TO YOU.** All you have to do is open your inbox and read.

☐ **EXCLUSIVE CONTENT.** We cover the news overlooked by the mainstream press.

☐ **STAY CURRENT.** Find the latest court rulings, revivals, and cultural trends.

☐ **UPDATE OTHERS.** Easy to forward to friends and family with the click of your mouse.

CHOOSE THE E-NEWSLETTER THAT INTERESTS YOU MOST:

- Christian news
- Daily devotionals
- Spiritual empowerment
- And much, much more

SIGN UP AT: **http://freenewsletters.charismamag.com**

8178